W9-AAU-837

ATTENTION-DEFICIT HYPERACTIVITY DISORDER

ATTENTION-DEFICIT HYPERACTIVITY DISORDER
A Clinical Workbook

Second Edition

Russell A. Barkley and Kevin R. Murphy

THE GUILFORD PRESS
New York   London

© 1998 The Guilford Press
A Division of Guilford Publications, Inc.
72 Spring Street, New York, NY 10012
http://www.guilford.com

All rights reserved

Except as noted, no part of this book may be reproduced, translated,
stored in a retrieval system, or transmitted, in any form or by any
means, electronic, mechanical, photocopying, microfilming, record-
ing, or otherwise, without written permission from the Publisher.

Printed in the United States of America

This book is printed on acid-free paper.

Last digit is print number: 9   8   7   6   5   4   3

LIMITED PHOTOCOPY LICENSE

These materials are intended for use only by qualified mental
health professionals.

The Publisher grants to individual purchasers of this book
nonassignable permission to reproduce handouts and forms in
this book for use with their own clients and patients. This
license is limited to the individual purchaser and does not
extend to additional clinicians or practice settings. The license
does not grant the right to reproduce these materials for resale,
redistribution, or any other purposes (including but not limited
to research, books, pamphlets, articles, video or audio tapes,
and handouts or slides for lectures or workshops). Permission to
reproduce these materials for these and any other purposes
must be obtained in writing from the Permissions Department at
Guilford Publications.

ISBN 1-57230-301-8

Preface

All the materials in this manual are intended to be of the utmost convenience and utility when employed in your clinical practice. These materials are meant to accompany Barkley's recently revised *Attention-Deficit Hyperactivity Disorder: A Handbook for Diagnosis and Treatment* (2nd ed., Guilford Press, 1998). We strongly recommend reading the *Handbook* before using the enclosed clinical tools in your practice.

We are most grateful to Michael Breen, PhD, and Thomas Altepeter, PhD, for their permission to once again reprint the norms for the Home and School Situations Questionnaires; to George DuPaul, PhD, and his colleagues for their permission to provide the clinical cutoff scores for the ADHD items on the Disruptive Behavior Rating Scales based on their normative study for that item set; and to Arthur Robin, PhD, for his continued permission to reprint the Issues Checklist in this manual.

RUSSELL A. BARKLEY, PhD
KEVIN R. MURPHY, PhD

Contents

Forms for Use during Medication Treatment

ADHD Fact Sheet

This fact sheet was developed by Barkley as a ready reference to be given to parents and teachers of children with Attention-Deficit/Hyperactivity Disorder (ADHD) or to adults who have been diagnosed with ADHD who have been seen in your clinical practice. It can be handed out as part of the feedback conference following your evaluation. Or, it can be mailed to a child's teachers at his or her school along with specific recommendations for classroom management of that child. In a similar fashion, it can be provided to the employer, supervisor, or family members of an adult diagnosed with ADHD, with that adult's permission, of course.

*   *   *

Attention-Deficit/Hyperactivity Disorder is the current term for a specific developmental disorder seen in both children and adults that comprises deficits in behavioral inhibition, sustained attention and resistance to distraction, and the regulation of one's activity level to the demands of a situation (hyperactivity or restlessness). This disorder has had numerous different labels over the past century, including hyperactive child syndrome, hyperkinetic reaction of childhood, minimal brain dysfunction, and attention deficit disorder (with or without hyperactivity).

Major Characteristics

The predominant features of this disorder include the following:

1. *Impaired response inhibition, impulse control, or the capacity to delay gratification.* These are often noted in the individual's inability to stop and think before acting; to wait one's turn while playing games, conversing with others, or having to wait in line; to interrupt

From *Attention-Deficit Hyperactivity Disorder: A Clinical Workbook* (2nd ed.) by Russell A. Barkley and Kevin R. Murphy. Copyright 1998 by The Guilford Press. Permission to photocopy this form is granted to purchasers of the *Workbook* for personal use only. See copyright page for details.

responding quickly when it becomes evident that the individual's actions are no longer effective; to resist distractions while concentrating or working; to work for larger, longer-term rewards rather than opting for smaller, more immediate ones; and to inhibit the dominant or immediate reaction to an event, as the situation may demand.

2. *Excessive task-irrelevant activity or activity poorly regulated to the demands of a situation.* Individuals with ADHD in many cases are noted to be excessively fidgety, restless, and "on the go." They display excessive movement not required to complete a task, such as wriggling their feet and legs, tapping things, rocking while seated, or shifting their posture or position while performing relatively boring tasks. Younger children with the disorder may show excessive running, climbing, and other gross motor activity. Although this tends to decline with age, even teenagers with ADHD are more restless and fidgety than their peers. In adults with the disorder, this restlessness may be more subjective than outwardly observable, although some adults remain outwardly restless as well and report a need to always be busy or doing something and being unable to sit still.

3. *Poor sustained attention or persistence of effort to tasks.* This problem often arises when the individual is assigned boring, tedious, protracted, or repetitive activities that lack intrinsic appeal to the person. Such individuals often fail to show the same level of persistence, "stick-to-it-tiveness," motivation, and willpower of others their age when uninteresting yet important tasks must be performed. They often report becoming easily bored with such tasks and consequently shift from one uncompleted activity to another without completing these activities. Loss of concentration during tedious, boring, or protracted tasks is commonplace, as is an inability to return to the task on which they were working should they be unexpectedly interrupted. Thus, they are easily distracted during periods when concentration is important to the task at hand. They may also have problems with completing routine assignments without direct supervision and being able to stay on task during independent work.

These are the three most common areas of difficulty associated with ADHD. However, research suggests that those with ADHD, particularly the subtypes associated with impulsive behavior (discussed later), may also have difficulties in the following areas of psychological functioning:

1. *Remembering to do things, or working memory.* Working memory refers to the capacity to hold information in mind that will be used to guide one's actions either now or at a later time. It is essential for remembering to do things in the near future. Those with ADHD often have difficulties with working memory and so are described as forgetful around doing things, unable to keep important information in mind that they will need to guide their actions later, and disorganized in their thinking and other activities as they often lose track of the goal of their activities. They may often be described as acting without hindsight or forethought and being less able to anticipate and prepare for future events as well as others are, all of which seem to depend on working memory. Recent research suggests that those with ADHD cannot sense or use time as adequately as others in their daily activities; thus

they are often late for appointments and deadlines, ill-prepared for upcoming activities, and less able to pursue long-term goals and plans. Problems with time management and organizing themselves for upcoming events are commonplace in older children and adults with the disorder.

2. *Delayed development of internal language (the mind's voice) and rule following.* Recent research suggests that children with ADHD are significantly delayed in the development of internal language—the private voice inside our mind that we employ to converse with ourselves, contemplate events, and direct or command our own behavior. This private speech is absolutely essential to the normal development of contemplation, reflection, and self-regulation. Its delay in those with ADHD contributes to significant problems with their ability to follow through on rules and instructions; to read and follow directions carefully; to follow through on their own plans, rules, and "do-lists"; and even to act with legal or moral principles in mind. When combined with their difficulties with working memory, this problem with self-talk or private speech often results in significant interference with reading comprehension, especially of complex, uninteresting, or extended reading assignments.

3. *Difficulties with regulation of emotions, motivation, and arousal.* Children and adults with ADHD often have problems inhibiting their emotional reactions to events as well as do others of their age. It is not that the emotions they experience are inappropriate but that those with ADHD are more likely to publicly manifest the emotions they experience than would someone else. They seem less able to "internalize" their feelings, to keep them to themselves, and even to moderate them when they do so as others might do. Consequently, they are likely to appear to others as less emotionally mature, more reactive with their feelings, and more hot-headed, quick-tempered, and easily frustrated by events. Coupled with this problem with emotion regulation is the difficulties they have in generating intrinsic motivation for tasks that have no immediate payoff or appeal to them. This capacity to create private motivation, drive, or determination often makes them appear to lack will-power or self-discipline as they cannot stay with things that do not provide immediate reward, stimulation, or interest to them. Their motivation remains dependent on the immediate environment for how hard and how long they will work, whereas others develop a capacity for intrinsically motivating themselves in the absence of immediate rewards or other consequences. Also related to these difficulties with regulating emotion and motivation is that of regulating their general level of arousal to meet situational demands. Those with ADHD find it difficult to activate or arouse themselves to initiate work that must be done, often complain of being unable to stay alert or even awake in boring situations, and frequently seem to be daydreamy or "in a fog" when they should be more alert, focused, and actively engaged in a task.

4. *Diminished problem-solving ability, ingenuity, and flexibility in pursuing long-term goals.* Oftentimes, when we are engaged in goal-directed activities, we encounter problems that are obstacles to the goal's attainment. At these times, individuals must be capable of quickly generating a variety of options to themselves, considering their respective outcomes, and selecting among them one that seems most likely to surmount the obstacle so they can

continue toward their goal. Persons with ADHD find such hurdles to their goals to be more difficult to surmount; they often give up their goals in the face of obstacles and do not take the time to think through other options that could help them succeed toward their goal. Thus they may appear as less flexible in approaching problem situations and more likely to respond automatically or on impulse, and so are less creative at overcoming the roadblocks to their goals than others are likely to be. These problems may even be evident in the speech and writing of those with the disorder, as they are less able to quickly assemble their ideas into a more organized, coherent explanation of their thoughts. Thus they are less able to rapidly assemble their actions or ideas into a chain of responses that effectively accomplishes the goal given them, be it verbal or behavioral in nature.

5. *Greater than normal variability in their task or work performance.* It is typical of those with ADHD, especially those subtypes associated with impulsive behavior, to show substantial variability across time in the performance of their work. These wide swings may be found in the quality, quantity, and even speed of their work. In addition, they fail to maintain a relatively even pattern of productivity and accuracy in their work from moment to moment and day to day. Such variability is often puzzling to others who witness it, as it is clear that at times a person with ADHD can complete his or her work quickly and correctly whereas other times his or her tasks are performed poorly, inaccurately, and quite erratically. Indeed, some researchers see this pattern of high variability in work-related activities to be as much a hallmark of the disorder as is the poor inhibition and inattention described above.

Other Characteristics

Several other developmental characteristics are associated with the disorder:

1. *Early onset of the major characteristics.* The symptoms of ADHD appear to arise, on average, between 3 and 6 years of age. This is particularly so for those subtypes of ADHD associated with hyperactive and impulsive behavior. Others may not develop their symptoms until somewhat later in childhood. But certainly the vast majority of those with the disorder have had some symptoms since before the age of 13. Those who have ADHD, Predominantly Inattentive Type, which is not associated with impulsiveness, appear to develop their attention problems somewhat later than do the other subtypes, often in middle or later childhood. Thus the disorder is believed to be one of childhood onset, regardless of the subtype, suggesting that should these symptoms develop for the first time in adulthood, other mental disorders rather than ADHD should be suspected.

2. *Situational variation of symptoms.* The major symptoms of ADHD are likely to change markedly as a consequence of the nature of the situation in which the person happens to be. Research suggests that those with ADHD behave better in one-to-one situations, when doing tasks that they enjoy or find interesting, when there is some immediate payoff for behaving well, when they are supervised, when their work is done earlier in the day rather than later, and, for children, when they are with their fathers compared to their mothers. Conversely, those with ADHD may manifest more of their symptoms in group settings,

when they must perform boring work, when they must work independently of supervision, when their work must be done later in the day, and (for children) when they are with their mothers. Sometimes, or in some cases, these situational factors may have little affect on the person's level of ADHD symptoms, but they have been noted often enough in research to make such situational changes in their symptoms important to appreciate.

3. *Relatively chronic course*. ADHD symptoms are often quite developmentally stable. Although the absolute level of symptoms does decline with age, this is true of the inattentiveness, impulsiveness, and activity levels of normal individuals as well. Thus those with ADHD may be improving in their behavior but not always catching up with their peer group in this regard. This seems to leave them chronically behind others of their age in their capacity to inhibit behavior, sustain attention, control distractibility, and regulate their activity level. Research suggests that among those children clinically diagnosed with the disorder in childhood, 50–80% will continue to meet the criteria for the diagnosis in adolescence, and 10–65% may continue to do so in adulthood. Whether or not they have the full syndrome in adulthood, at least 50–70% may continue to manifest some symptoms that are causing them some impairment in their adult life.

Adult Outcome

It has been estimated that anywhere from 15% to 50% of those with ADHD ultimately outgrow the disorder. However, these figures come from follow-up studies in which the current and more rigorous diagnostic criteria for the disorder were not used. When more appropriate and modern criteria are employed, probably only 20–35% of children with the disorder no longer have any symptoms resulting in impairment in their adult life. Over the course of their lives, a significant minority of those with ADHD experience a greater risk for developing oppositional and defiant behavior (>50%), conduct problems and antisocial difficulties (25–45%), learning disabilities (25–40%), low self-esteem, and depression (25%). Approximately 5–10% of those with ADHD may develop more serious mental disorders, such as manic–depression. Between 10% and 20% may develop antisocial personality disorder by adulthood, most of whom will also have problems with substance abuse. Overall, approximately 10–25% develop difficulties with overuse, dependence on, or even abuse of legal (e.g., alcohol and tobacco) or illegal (e.g., marijuana, cocaine, and illicit use of prescription drugs) substances, with this risk being greatest among those who had conduct disorder or delinquency as adolescents. Despite these risks, upwards of half or more of those who have ADHD do not develop these associated difficulties or disorders. However, the majority of those with ADHD certainly experienced problems with school performance, with as many as 30–50% having been retained in their school grade at least once, and 25–36% never completing high school.

As adults, those with ADHD are likely to be undereducated relative to their intellectual ability and family educational background. They are also likely to experience difficulties with work adjustment and may be underemployed in their occupations relative to their intelligence and educational and family backgrounds. They tend to change their jobs more often than others do, sometimes out of boredom or because of interpersonal problems in the workplace. They also tend to have a greater turnover of friendships and dating relationships and seem more prone to marital discord and even divorce. Difficulties with speeding while driving are relatively commonplace, as are more traffic citations for this behavior, and, in some cases, more motor vehicle accidents than others are likely to experience in their driving careers. Thus, they are more likely to have had their driver's license suspended or revoked.

Subtypes

Since 1980, it has become possible to place those with ADHD into several subtypes, depending on the combinations of symptoms they experience. Those who have difficulties primarily with impulsive and hyperactive behavior and not with attention or concentration are now referred to as having ADHD, Predominantly Hyperactive–Impulsive Type. Individuals with the opposite pattern, significant inattentiveness without being impulsive or hyperactive are called ADHD, Predominantly Inattentive Type. However, most individuals with the disorder will manifest both of these clinical features and thus are referred to as ADHD, Combined Type. Research on those with the Combined Type suggests that they are likely to develop their hyperactive and/or impulsive symptoms first and usually during the preschool years. At this age, then, they may be diagnosed as having the Predominantly Hyperactive–Impulsive Type. However, in most of these cases, they eventually progress to developing the difficulties with attention span, persistence, and distractibility within a few years of entering school and are then diagnosed as having the Combined Type.

There is considerably less research on ADHD, Predominantly Inattentive Type, or what used to be referred to as Attention Deficit Disorder without Hyperactivity. What research does exist suggests some qualitative differences between the attention problems these individuals experience and those with the other types of ADHD in which hyperactive or impulsive behavior is present. ADHD, Predominantly Inattentive Type appears to be associated with more daydreaming, passiveness, sluggishness, difficulties with focused or selective attention (filtering important from unimportant information), slow processing of information, mental fogginess and confusion, social quietness or apprehensiveness, hypoactivity, and inconsistent retrieval of information from memory. It is also considerably less likely to be associated with impulsiveness (by definition) as well as oppositional–defiant behavior, conduct problems, or delinquency. Should further research continue to demonstrate such differences, there would be good reason to view this subtype as actually a separate and distinct disorder from that of ADHD.

Prevalence

ADHD occurs in approximately 3–7% of the childhood population and approximately 2–5% of the adult population. Among children the gender ratio is approximately 3:1 with boys more likely to have the disorder than girls. Among adults, the gender ratio falls to 2:1 or lower. The disorder has been found to exist in virtually every country in which it has been investigated, including North America, South America, Great Britain, Scandinavia, Europe, Japan, China, Turkey, and the Middle East. The disorder may not be referred to as ADHD in these countries and may not be treated in the same fashion as in North America, but there is little doubt that the disorder is virtually universal among human populations. The disorder is more likely to be found in families in which others have the disorder or where depression is more common. It is also more likely to occur in those with conduct problems and delinquency, tic disorders or Tourette syndrome, learning disabilities, or those with a history of prenatal alcohol or tobacco-smoke exposure, premature delivery or significantly low birth weight, or significant trauma to the frontal regions of the brain.

Etiologies

ADHD has very strong biological contributions to its occurrence. Although precise causes have not yet been identified, there is little question that heredity/genetics makes the largest contribution to the expression of the disorder in the population. The heritability of ADHD averages approximately 80%, meaning that genetic factors account for 80% of the differences among individuals in this set of behavioral traits. For comparison, consider that this figure rivals that for the role of genetics in human height. Researchers have identified several genes associated with the disorder, and undoubtedly they will identify more given that ADHD represents a set of complex behavioral traits and thus a single gene is unlikely to account for the disorder. In instances in which heredity does not seem to be a factor, difficulties during pregnancy, prenatal exposure to alcohol and tobacco smoke, prematurity of delivery and significantly low birth weight, and excessively high body lead levels, as well as postnatal injury to the prefrontal regions of the brain, have all been found to contribute to the risk for the disorder in varying degrees. Research does not support popularly held views that ADHD arises from excessive sugar intake, food additives, excessive viewing of television, or poor child management by parents. Some drugs used to treat seizure disorders in children may have side effects that increase symptoms of ADHD in those children, but these effects are reversible.

Treatment

No treatments have been found to cure this disorder, but many treatments exist which can effectively assist with its management. Chief among these treatments is the education of the family and school staff about the nature of the disorder and its management, in the case of children with the disorder, and the education and counseling of the adult with ADHD and their family members. But among the treatments that result in the greatest degree of improvement in the symptoms of the disorder, research overwhelmingly supports the use of the stimulant medications for this disorder (e.g., methylphenidate [Ritalin], D-amphetamine [Dexedrine], a combination of different forms of amphetamine [Adderall], and, in rare cases, pemoline [Cylert]). Evidence also shows that the tricyclic antidepressants, in particular desipramine, may also be effective in managing symptoms of the disorder as well as coexisting symptoms of mood disorder or anxiety. However, these antidepressants do not appear to be as effective as the stimulants. Research evidence is rather mixed on whether or not clonidine is of specific benefit for management of these symptoms apart from its well-known sedation effects. A small percentage of individuals with ADHD may require combinations of these medications, or others, for the management of their disorder, often because of the coexistence of other mental disorders with their ADHD.

Psychological treatments, such as behavior modification in the classroom and parent training in child behavior management methods, have been shown to produce short-term benefits in these settings. However, the improvements they render are often limited to those settings in which treatment is occurring and do not generalize to other settings that are not included in the management program. Moreover, recent studies suggest, as with the medications discussed above, that the gains obtained during treatment may not last once treatment has been terminated. Thus, it appears that treatments for ADHD must often be combined and must be maintained over long periods to sustain the initial treatment effects. In this regard, ADHD should be viewed like any other chronic medical condition that requires ongoing treatment for its effective management but whose treatments do not rid the individual of the disorder. Some children with ADHD may benefit from social skills training provided it is incorporated into their school program. Children with ADHD are now eligible for special educational services in the public schools under both the Individuals with Disabilities in Education Act (IDEA; Public Law 101-476) and Section 504 of the Rehabilitation Act of 1973 (Public Law 93-112).

Adults with ADHD are also eligible for accommodations in their workplace or educational settings under the Americans with Disabilities Act provided that the severity of their ADHD is such that it produces impairments in one or more major areas of life functioning and that they disclose their disorder to their employer or educational institution. Adults with the disorder may also require counseling about their condition, vocational assessment and counseling to find the most suitable work environment, time management and organizational assistance, and other suggestions for coping with their disorder. The medications noted previously that are useful for children with ADHD have recently proven to be as effective in the management of ADHD in adults.

Treatments with little or no evidence for their effectiveness include dietary management, such as removal of sugar from the diet, high doses of vitamins, minerals, trace elements, or other popular health food remedies, long-term psychotherapy or psychoanalysis, biofeedback, play therapy, chiropractic treatment, or sensory-integration training, despite the widespread popularity of some of these treatment approaches.

The treatment of ADHD requires a comprehensive behavioral, psychological, educational, and sometimes medical evaluation followed by education of the individual or his or her family members as to the nature of the disorder and the methods proven to assist with its management. Treatment is likely to be multidisciplinary, requiring the assistance of the mental health, educational, and medical professions at various points in its course. Treatment must be provided over long periods to assist those with ADHD in the ongoing management of their disorder. In so doing, many with the disorder can lead satisfactory, reasonably adjusted, and productive lives.

Forms for Use with Children and Adolescents

Instructions for Child and Adolescent Forms

The following clinical intake and interview forms are intended for use in conjunction with the chapter on interviewing parents of children and adolescents with ADHD from my (Barkley) recent text, *Attention-Deficit Hyperactivity Disorder: A Handbook for Diagnosis and Treatment* (2nd ed., Guilford Press, 1998).

Clinical Intake Forms

The three clinical intake forms (General Instructions for Completing the Questionnaires, Child and Family Information, and Developmental and Medical History) can be sent to parents to complete and return in advance of their child's appointment with you for their evaluation. You may also wish to send out the Disruptive Behavior Rating Scale (DBRS) and Home Situations Questionnaire (HSQ) to parents in this same packet of materials. I strongly advise that you also include in this packet a broad-band rating scale covering the major dimensions of child psychopathology, such as the Child Behavior Checklist (Acherbach, 1991), Behavioral Assessment System for Children (Reynolds & Kamphaus, 1994), or Conners Parent Questionnaire (Conners, 1997). You may also wish to include the pamphlet provided here on How to Prepare for Your Child's Evaluation. Of course, this assumes that the information provided here to parents about the nature of the evaluation corresponds to the manner in which you conduct such evaluations. There is also a school version of the DBRS and the School Situations Questionnaire (SSQ) that can be sent to teachers to complete and return in advance of the appointment. Again, we strongly encourage the inclusion in this packet of a broad-band rating scale like those listed previously.

Clinical Interview—Parent Report Form

The parental interview form contains questions pertaining to the child's reason for referral, developmental, medical, social, and educational history, as well as the symptoms of most of the major childhood mental disorders likely to be seen in the evaluation of children and adolescents for this disorder. Those symptom lists and diagnostic criteria are taken from the fourth edition of the *Diagnostic and Statistical Manual of Mental Disorders* (DSM-IV; American Psychiatric Association, 1994) and have been adapted here with permission of the American Psychiatric Association. This interview can be used for both clinical or research purposes in interviewing parents of children or teenagers being evaluated for ADHD.

Scoring the Disruptive Behavior Rating Scales

The DBRS contains the symptoms for ADHD, Oppositional Defiant, and Conduct Disorder (parent form only) as they appear in DSM-IV. The teacher form of this scale does not include the items for Conduct Disorder as teachers are likely to have far less information about these activities than do parents.

Odd-numbered items (1, 3, 5, 7, 9, 11, . . .) are from the Inattention symptom list for ADHD; even-numbered items (2, 4, 6, 8, . . .) are from the Hyperactive–Impulsive symptom list for ADHD. Items 19–26 are from the symptom list for Oppositional Defiant Disorder (ODD). On the parent form, the remaining 15 Yes–No items are the symptom list for Conduct Disorder. To score the ADHD items, sum the odd-numbered item scores for the Inattention items (1, 3, 5, 7, 9, 11, 13, 15, 17) separately. Do the same for the even numbered Hyperactive–Impulsive items (2, 4, 6, 8, 10, 12, 14, 16, 18). Then consult the cutoff scores below for these ADHD items. To score the ODD items (19–26), simply count the number of items answered either 2 (often) or 3 (very often). If the number is 4 or more, this meets or exceeds the recommended symptom cutoff threshold for ODD in DSM-IV. Norms are *not* available for this list of symptoms. To score the items for Conduct Disorder, simply count the number of items answered Yes. If three or more of these items have been so answered, this meets the symptom threshold for Conduct Disorder as established in the DSM-IV. Again norms are not available for these items but none are really necessary, as the occurrence of just a few of these activities by a child can be developmentally deviant.

The school version of the DBRS is scored the same way except that no Conduct Disorder items are on that version of the scale.

Norms for the ADHD items in this scale have recently been collected by George DuPaul and colleagues for these ADHD items (DuPaul et al., 1997, in press). A separate manual containing a separate ADHD Rating Scale along with the full report on these norms and the psychometric properties of this scale by Dr. DuPaul and his colleagues is available from Guilford Press.

To score the ADHD items in the DBRS provided here, the clinician would add up *the total points* circled for all the items (including answers of 0's, and 1's) on the Inattention and Hyperactive–Impulsive lists separately. The 93rd percentile has typically been construed

Clinical Cutoff Scores for ADHD Items

Age groups (in years)	Boys		Girls	
	Inattention	Hyper.–Imp.	Inattention	Hyper.–Imp.
Parent ratings				
5–7	15	17	12	13
8–10	15	15	12	9
11–13	18.5	16	12.8	9
Teacher ratings				
5–7	22	22	21	21
8–10	25	25	21	16.7
11–13	24	18	19	14.8

as reflecting clinical significance, and so, with permission of the authors of this scale, we provide in the accompanying table the thresholds for the 93rd percentile for these scores for each of these lists given separately by source of report, child age and child gender.

Scoring the Home and School Situations Questionnaires

The HSQ and SSQ evaluate the pervasiveness and severity of children's behavior problems across multiple home and school situations. On the HSQ, parents rate their child's behavioral problems across 16 different home and public situations. On the SSQ, teachers report on the problems children may have in 12 different school situations. Both scales are scored the same way to yield two separate scores. The first is the Number of Problem Settings, calculated simply by counting the number of items answered Yes. The second is the Mean Severity, calculated by summing the numbers circled beside the items and then dividing by the number of Yes answers. Again, using the 93rd percentile (+1.5 standard deviations above the mean) as an indication of clinical significance, scores at or above that threshold would be significant. The norms for these rating scales are presented in the tables on page 14.

Issues Checklist for Parents and Teenagers*

This scale was developed by Arthur Robin, PhD, and Sharon Foster, PhD, to assess the intensity of conflicts that adolescents have with their parents. Such information is very

*Adapted from *Dictionary of Behavioral Assessment* (pp. 278–279), M. Hersen & A. S. Bellack, Eds., New York, Pergamon Press, 1988. Copyright 1988 by Pergamon Press. Adapted by permission of the publisher.

Norms for the Home Situations Questionnaire

Age groups (in years)	N	Number of problem settings			Mean severity		
		Mean	SD	+1.5 SD	Mean	SD	+1.5 SD
Boys							
4–5	162	3.1	2.8	7.3	1.7	1.4	3.8
6–8	205	4.1	3.3	9.1	2.0	1.4	4.1
9–11	138	3.6	3.3	8.6	1.9	1.5	4.2
Girls							
4–5	146	2.2	2.6	6.1	1.3	1.4	3.4
6–8	202	3.4	3.5	8.7	1.6	1.5	3.9
9–11	142	2.7	3.2	7.5	1.4	1.4	3.5

Note. N, sample size at this age for this gender; *SD*, standard deviation; +1.5 *SD*, score at the threshold of 1.5 standard deviations above the mean (approximately the 93rd percentile). From Breen and Altepeter (1991). Copyright 1991 by Plenum Publishing Corp. Reprinted by permission of the authors and publisher.

Norms for the School Situations Questionnaire

Age groups (in years)	N	Number of problem settings			Mean severity		
		Mean	SD	+1.5 SD	Mean	SD	+1.5 SD
Boys							
6–8	170	2.4	3.3	7.4	1.5	2.0	4.5
9–11	123	2.8	3.2	7.6	1.9	2.1	5.1
Girls							
6–8	180	1.0	2.0	4.0	0.8	1.5	3.1
9–11	126	1.3	2.1	4.5	0.8	1.2	2.6

N, sample size at this age for this gender; *SD*, standard deviation; +1.5 *SD*, score at the threshold of 1.5 standard deviations above the mean (approximately the 93rd percentile). From Breen and Altepeter (1991). Copyright 1991 by Plenum Publishing Corp. Reprinted by permission of the authors and publisher.

helpful in tailoring a family therapy program to the needs of a particular family and in monitoring the effectiveness of therapy. The scoring instructions and norms are contained on pages 17–18.

Deviant scores are considered to be 1.5 to 2 standard deviations above the mean. However, even if the scores are not deviant, parents and teens may still be sufficiently concerned about particular communication problems and conflicts to require some type of intervention.

For a treatment approach, we recommend the Robin and Foster treatment program for parent–adolescent conflicts entitled Problem-Solving Communication Training. It can be obtained in their book, *Negotiating Parent–Adolescent Conflict* (Robin & Foster, 1989).

The program by Marion Forgatch and Gerald Patterson, *Parents and Adolescents Living Together* is similar and also excellent.

Description

The Issues Checklist (IC) assesses self-reports of specific disputes between parents and teenagers (Prinz, Foster, Kent, & O'Leary, 1979). It consists of a list of 44 issues that can lead to disagreements between parents and adolescents, such as chores, curfew, bedtime, friends, and homework. Parents and adolescents complete identical versions of the IC. Adolescents in two-parent families complete it separately for disputes with their mothers and fathers.

For each topic, the respondent indicates whether the issue has been broached during the previous 2 weeks. For each topic reported as having been discussed, the respondent rates the actual intensity of the discussions on a 5-point scale ranging from calm to angry and estimates how often the topics come up. The IC yields three scores for each respondent: (1) the quantity of issues (the total number of issues checked as broached); (2) the anger-intensity of issues (an average of the anger-intensity ratings for all of the endorsed issues); and (3) the weighted average of the frequency and anger-intensity level of issues (a score obtained by multiplying each frequency estimate by its associated intensity, summing these cross products, then dividing by the total of all the frequency estimates). The weighted average provides an estimate of the anger *per discussion*, whereas the intensity score reflects the average anger *per issue*, regardless of the frequency with which the issue was discussed.

Purpose

The IC is designed to provide scientific information regarding the frequency and content of disputes between parents and adolescents and the perceived anger-intensity level of these disputes. It covers a broad array of possible disputes applicable to 12- to 16-year-old teenagers and their parents.

Development

The IC was constructed by revising a similar instrument developed by Robin, with issues selected based on literature on parent–adolescent relationships and clinical experience. No pilot testing was done prior to formal validation studies.

Psychometric Characteristics

The reliability, discriminant/criterion-related validity, and treatment sensitivity of the IC has been examined in a number of investigations. Estimates of test–retest reliability were computed in two studies. Using small sample data collected over 6- to 8-week intervals from the wait-list groups of two outcome studies (Foster, Prinz, & O'Leary, 1983; Robin, 1981), adolescent reliability ranged from .49 to .87 for the quantity of issues, .37 to .49 for the anger-intensity score, and .15 to .24 for the weighted frequency by intensity score. Parental reliability was higher, averaging .65 and .55 for mother and father quantity of issues, .81 and .66 for mother and father anger-intensity scores, and .90 and .40 for mother and father weighted frequency by anger-intensity scores. Using 33 nonclinic families assessed over 1- to 2-week intervals, Enyart (1984) found somewhat higher reliabilities, particularly for adolescents (range = .49–.80).

Agreement reliability between mothers and adolescents, assessed by examining whether parents and adolescents concurred that an issue either had or had not been discussed, averaged 68% (range = 38–86%). When the congruence of mother and adolescent responses was examined via correlations, results ranged from .10 to .64 (mean r = .28). These results may raise questions about the accuracy of the IC as a measure of actual discussions at home or of the recall of one or both people.

The discriminant/criterion-related validity of the IC has been studied by contrasting the responses of distressed parents and adolescents (referred for treatment of family relationship problems) with the responses of nondistressed parents and teenagers (no history of treatment and self-reports of satisfactory relationships). Aggregated data from three assessment and two treatment studies with adolescents ages 10–18, male and female, revealed that all the IC scores discriminated between groups, with the most pronounced effects on maternal anger-intensity scores (accounting for 48% of the variance in distress/nondistressed status) and paternal quantity of issues scores (36% of the variance) (Robin & Foster, 1984). Adolescent effects were much weaker, explaining 3–19% of the variance (mean = 12%). Across all scores, distressed family members reported significantly more frequent, angrier disputes than nondistressed family members.

When the IC was used as a pre–post measure of change, treatment outcome studies of both a problem-solving communication skill training program and a heterogeneous non-behavioral family therapy revealed significant decrements in anger-intensity and weighted frequency by anger-intensity scores following intervention (Foster et al., 1983; Robin, 1981).

Clinical Use

The clinician can use the IC to pinpoint sources of conflict and survey which topics are perceived as provoking the greatest amounts of anger. These topics ordinarily are selected by family members as their most important problems and often warrant further assessment via interviews and/or home data collection. Ratings of IC issues can also help the therapist sequence a skill-oriented treatment so that early intervention sessions focus on less intense conflicts and later sessions address more intense problems. Noting discrepancies between parent and adolescent ICs and inquiring further about them can also yield invaluable information about differential perceptions within the family system. Preliminary norms from distressed and nondistressed families are also available (Robin & Foster, 1984). Because the IC was validated on families with adolescents experiencing externalizing behavior disorders (Attention Deficit Disorder, Conduct Disorder, etc.), its psychometric properties with families in which the adolescents have other presenting problems are unknown. Thus, it should be interpreted cautiously with such populations.

Future Directions

The most important unanswered question concerning the IC is the extent to which reports of specific disputes correspond to actual disputes. The low reliability suggests that the IC may not be an accurate measure of actual interactions. Correlational studies comparing retrospective IC scores to daily reports and direct observations of family disputes are needed. In addition, a broader-based normative sample including distressed families with a variety of presenting problems would be desirable.

Scoring Instructions

This is a measure of the frequency and anger-intensity level of specific disputes between parents and teenagers. Three scores are computed as indicated below, and the results can be compared to normative data to make inferences about the level of specific disputes for a given family.

1. *Quantity of issue.* Sum the number of issues checked Yes.
2. *Anger-intensity level of issues.* For issues checked Yes, sum the intensity ratings and divide by the number of issues checked Yes to obtain a mean anger-intensity score.
3. *Weighted frequency by anger-intensity level of issues.*
    a. Multiply each frequency by its associated anger-intensity score.
    b. Sum the products of each intensity times frequency.
    c. Sum the frequencies.
    d. Divide the sum of the products by the sum of the frequencies.

Norms for the Issues Checklist

	Distressed			Nondistressed				
	n	$\bar{x}$	SD	n	$\bar{x}$	SD	t	$r_{pbs}{}^a$
Maternal quantity	124	22.55	7.35	68	17.83	7.07	3.62**	.25
Maternal anger intensity	124	2.42	0.46	68	1.70	0.45	11.43**	.64
Maternal anger intensity × frequency	124	2.29	2.15	68	0.83	1.08	5.21**	.35
Adolescent–mother quantity	96	20.68	7.59	68	18.46	7.25	1.88*	.15
Adolescent–mother anger intensity	96	2.34	0.63	68	1.77	0.49	6.20**	.44
Adolescent–mother anger intensity × frequency	96	1.93	1.81	68	0.84	0.86	4.60**	.40
Paternal quantity	60	18.38	5.05	38	11.64	4.63	6.61**	.60

(cont.)

	Distressed			Nondistressed				
	n	$\bar{x}$	SD	n	$\bar{x}$	SD	t	$r_{pbs}{}^a$
Paternal anger intensity	60	2.18	0.60	38	1.82	0.57	2.93*	.29
Paternal anger intensity × frequency	60	2.39	0.64	38	1.94	0.59	3.46**	.33
Adolescent–father quantity	38	13.60	5.54	14	10.71	4.65	1.71 *	.24
Adolescent–father anger intensity	38	2.40	0.76	14	1.75	0.64	2.80*	.37
Adolescent–father anger intensity × frequency	38	2.72	0.95	14	1.88	0.69	2.97*	.39

Note. From *Negotiating Parent–Adolescent Conflict* by A. L. Robin and S. L. Foster. Copyright 1989 by The Guilford Press. Reprinted by permission.

$^a r_{pbs}$, point-biserial correlation between the particular score and group membership (distressed vs. nondistressed).

* $p < .05$.
** $p < .001$.

Daily School Behavior Report Cards

Children and teens with ADHD often have considerable problems with behavior in the school setting. To assist parents with improving their child's school behavior, I have invented three different forms of the Daily School Report Cards and included them here, along with instructions to parents on how to employ these cards.

References

American Psychiatric Association. (1994). *Diagnostic and statistical manual of mental disorders* (4th ed.). Washington, DC: Author.

Achenbach, T. M. (1991). *Manual for the Child Behavior Checklist/4-18 and 1991 Profile.* Burlington: University of Vermont, Department of Psychiatry.

Breen, M. J., & Altepeter, T. S. (1991). Factor structure of the Home Situations Questionnaire and the School Situations Questionnaire. *Journal of Pediatric Psychology, 16*, 50–67.

Conners, C. K. (1997). *The New Conners Rating Scales.* North Tonawanda, NY: Multi-Health Systems.

DuPaul, G. J., Anastopoulos, A. D., Power, T. J., Reid, R., Ikeda, M. J., & McGoey, K. E. (in press). Parent ratings of attention-deficit/hyperactivity disorder symptoms: Factor structure, normative data, and psychometric properties. *Journal of Psychoeducational Assessment.*

DuPaul, G. J., Power, T. J., Anastopoulos, A. D., Reid, R., McGoey, K. E., & Ikeda, M. J. (1997). Teacher ratings of attention-deficit/hyperactivity disorder symptoms: Factor structure, normative data, and psychometric properties. *Psychological Assessment, 9,* 436–444.

Enyart, P. (1984). *Behavioral correlates of self-reported parent–adolescent relationship satisfaction.* Unpublished doctoral dissertation, West Virginia University, Morgantown.

Forgatch, M., Patterson, G. (1989). *Parents and adolescents living together.* Eugene, OR: Castalia Press.

Foster, S. L., Prinz, R. J, & O Leary, K. D. (1983). Impact of problem-solving communication training and generalization procedures on family conflict. *Child and Family Behavior Therapy, 5,* 1–23.

Prinz, R. J., Foster, S. L., Kent, R. N., & O'Leary, K. D. (1983). Multivariate assessment of conflict in distressed and nondistressed mother–adolescent dyads. *Journal of Applied Behavior Analysis, 12,* 691–700.

Reynolds, C., & Kamphaus, R. (1994). *Behavioral Assessment System for Children.* Circle Pines, MN: American Guidance Service.

Robin, A. L. (1981). A controlled evaluation of problem-solving communication training with parent–adolescent conflict. *Behavior Therapy, 12,* 593–609.

Robin, A. L., & Foster, S. L. (1984). Problem solving communication training: A behavioral–family systems approach to parent–adolescent conflict. In P. Karoly & J. J. Steffen (Eds.), *Adolescent behavior disorders: Foundations and contemporary concerns* (pp. 195–240). Lexington, MA: Heath.

Robin, A. L., & Foster, S. L. (1989). *Negotiating parent–adolescent conflict: A behavioral–family systems approach.* New York: Guilford Press.

GENERAL INSTRUCTIONS FOR COMPLETING THE QUESTIONNAIRES

As part of processing your request for an evaluation of your child at our clinic, we must ask you to complete the enclosed forms about your child and your family. We greatly appreciate your willingness to complete these forms. Your answers will give us a much better understanding of your child's behavior at home and your family circumstances. In completing these forms, please follow these instructions as closely as possible:

1. *All* forms in this packet should be completed by the parent who has the primary responsibility for caring for this child. Where both parents reside with the child, this is to be the parent who spends the greatest amount of time with the child.

2. If a second parent wishes to complete a second packet of information about this child, he/she may do so independently by requesting a second set of these forms. He/she may call our administrative assistant, _____, at _____ (phone), and the packet will be sent out promptly.

3. If your child is already taking medication for assistance with his/her behavior management (such as Ritalin) or for any emotional difficulties (such as an antidepressant), we must ask that you complete the questionnaires about your child's behavior *based on how your child behaves when he/she is OFF this medication*. It is very likely that you occasionally observe your child's behavior at periods when he/she is off of this medication, and we want you to use those time periods to answer these questions about behavior. In this way, we can get a clearer idea of the true nature of your child's difficulties without the alterations produced by any medication treatments being used. However, some parents whose children have been on medication for a long time may not be able to give us this information. In that case, just complete the questionnaires based on your child's behavior, but check the third blank line below to let us know that you based your judgments on your child's behavior when he/she was on medication. Check one of the blanks below to let us know for certain on what basis you judged your child's behavior in answering our behavior questionnaires:

   ____ My child currently does *not* take any medication for behavior problems. My answers are based on my child's behavior while he/she is off of medication.
   ____ My child *is currently taking medication* for behavior problems. However, my answers are based on my child's behavior while he/she is *OFF* of this medication.
   ____ My child *is currently taking medication* for behavior problems. My answers are based on my child's behavior while he/she is *ON* this medication.

Please list any medications your child is currently taking for behavioral or emotional difficulties:

_____

Thank you for completing these forms and returning them promptly to us in the enclosed envelope.

PLEASE RETURN THIS FORM ALONG WITH THE COMPLETED QUESTIONNAIRES.

From *Defiant Children* (2nd ed.): *A Clinician's Manual for Assessment and Parent Training* by Russell A. Barkley. Copyright 1997 by The Guilford Press. Reprinted in *Attention-Deficit Hyperactivity Disorder: A Clinical Workbook* (2nd ed.) by Russell A. Barkley and Kevin R. Murphy. Permission to photocopy this form is granted to purchasers of the *Workbook* for personal use only (see copyright page for details).

CHILD AND FAMILY INFORMATION

Child's name _____ **Birthdate** _____ **Age** _____

Address _____
                 (Street)   (City)   (State)   (Zip)

Home phone ( ) _____ Work phone ( ) _____ Dad/Mom
                                                                    (Circle one)

Child's school _____ Teacher's name _____

School address _____
                      (Street)   (City)   (State)   (Zip)

School phone ( ) _____ Child's grade _____

Is child in special education? Yes No If so, what type? _____

Father's name _____ Age _____ Education _____

Father's place of employment _____
                                                               (Years)

Type of employment _____ Annual salary _____

Mother's name _____ Age _____ Education _____

Mother's place of employment _____
                                                               (Years)

Type of employment _____ Annual salary _____

Is child adopted? Yes No If yes, age when adopted_____

Are parents married? Yes No Separated? Yes No Divorced? Yes No

Child's physician _____

Physician's address_____
                    (Street)   (City)   (State)   (Zip)

Physician's telephone number_____

Please list all other children in the family:

Name	Age	School grade

From *Defiant Children* (2nd ed.): *A Clinician's Manual for Assessment and Parent Training* by Russell A. Barkley. Copyright 1997 by The Guilford Press. Reprinted in *Attention-Deficit Hyperactivity Disorder: A Clinical Workbook* (2nd ed.) by Russell A. Barkley and Kevin R. Murphy. Permission to photocopy this form is granted to purchasers of the *Workbook* for personal use only (see copyright page for details).

DEVELOPMENTAL AND MEDICAL HISTORY

PREGNANCY AND DELIVERY

A. Length of pregnancy (e.g., full term, 40 weeks, 32 weeks, etc.) _____
B. Length of delivery (number of hours from initial labor pains to birth) _____
C. Mother's age when child was born _____
D. Child's birth weight _____
E. Did any of the following conditions occur during pregnancy/delivery?

1. Bleeding	No	Yes
2. Excessive weight gain (more than 30 lbs.)	No	Yes
3. Toxemia/preeclampsia	No	Yes
4. Rh factor incompatibility	No	Yes
5. Frequent nausea or vomiting	No	Yes
6. Serious illness or injury	No	Yes
7. Took prescription medications a. If yes, name of medication _____	No	Yes
8. Took illegal drugs	No	Yes
9. Used alcoholic beverage a. If yes, approximate number of drinks per week _____	No	Yes

10. Smoked cigarettes
   a. If yes, approximate number of cigarettes per day
   (e.g., ½ pack) _____
	No	Yes

11. Was given medication to ease labor pains a. If yes, name of medication _____	No	Yes
12. Delivery was induced	No	Yes
13. Forceps were used during delivery	No	Yes
14. Had a breech delivery	No	Yes
15. Had a cesarean section delivery	No	Yes
16. Other problems—please describe	No	Yes

F. Did any of the following conditions affect your child
during delivery or within the first few days after birth?

1. Injured during delivery	No	Yes
2. Cardiopulmonary distress during delivery	No	Yes

(cont.)

From *Defiant Children* (2nd ed.): *A Clinician's Manual for Assessment and Parent Training* by Russell A. Barkley. Copyright 1997 by The Guilford Press. Reprinted in *Attention-Deficit Hyperactivity Disorder: A Clinical Workbook* (2nd ed.) by Russell A. Barkley and Kevin R. Murphy. Permission to photocopy this form is granted to purchasers of the *Workbook* for personal use only (see copyright page for details).

3. Delivered with cord around neck	No	Yes
4. Had trouble breathing following delivery	No	Yes
5. Needed oxygen	No	Yes
6. Was cyanotic, turned blue	No	Yes
7. Was jaundiced, turned yellow	No	Yes
8. Had an infection	No	Yes
9. Had seizures	No	Yes
10. Was given medications	No	Yes
11. Born with a congenital defect	No	Yes
12. Was in hospital more than 7 days	No	Yes

INFANT HEALTH AND TEMPERAMENT

A. During the first 12 months, was your child:

1. Difficult to feed	No	Yes
2. Difficult to get to sleep	No	Yes
3. Colicky	No	Yes
4. Difficult to put on a schedule	No	Yes
5. Alert	No	Yes
6. Cheerful	No	Yes
7. Affectionate	No	Yes
8. Sociable	No	Yes
9. Easy to comfort	No	Yes
10. Difficult to keep busy	No	Yes
11. Overactive, in constant motion	No	Yes
12. Very stubborn, challenging	No	Yes

EARLY DEVELOPMENTAL MILESTONES

A. At what age did your child first accomplish the following:
  1. Sitting without help   _____
  2. Crawling   _____
  3. Walking alone, without assistance   _____
  4. Using single words (e.g.,"mama," "dada", "ball," etc.)   _____
  5. Putting two or more words together (e.g.,"mama up")   _____

(cont.)

6. Bowel training, day and night   _____
7. Bladder training, day and night   _____

HEALTH HISTORY

A. Date of child's last physical exam: _____

B. At any time has your child had the following:

1. Asthma	Never	Past	Present
2. Allergies	Never	Past	Present
3. Diabetes, arthritis, or other chronic illnesses	Never	Past	Present
4. Epilepsy or seizure disorder	Never	Past	Present
5. Febrile seizures	Never	Past	Present
6. Chicken pox or other common childhood illnesses	Never	Past	Present
7. Heart or blood pressure problems	Never	Past	Present
8. High fevers (over 103°)	Never	Past	Present
9. Broken bones	Never	Past	Present
10. Severe cuts requiring stitches	Never	Past	Present
11. Head injury with loss of consciousness	Never	Past	Present
12. Lead poisoning	Never	Past	Present
13. Surgery	Never	Past	Present
14. Lengthy hospitalization	Never	Past	Present
15. Speech or language problems	Never	Past	Present
16. Chronic ear infections	Never	Past	Present
17. Hearing difficulties	Never	Past	Present
18. Eye or vision problems	Never	Past	Present
19. Fine motor/handwriting problems	Never	Past	Present
20. Gross motor difficulties, clumsiness	Never	Past	Present
21. Appetite problems (overeating or undereating)	Never	Past	Present
22. Sleep problems (falling asleep, staying asleep)	Never	Past	Present
23. Soiling problems	Never	Past	Present
24. Wetting problems	Never	Past	Present

25. Other health difficulties—please describe

_____

HOW TO PREPARE FOR YOUR CHILD'S EVALUATION

Taking your child to a mental health professional for an evaluation is a major decision for any parent. Many parents do not know what to expect from such an evaluation and what they can do to be well prepared for it. That is why we are sending this pamphlet to you. It will give you some idea of how to prepare for your child's evaluation so that the time you spend with the professional can be used to its maximum advantage.

GETTING READY

In deciding to seek our professional help, consider what your concerns are at the moment. Typically, these concerns reflect problems with your child's behavioral, emotional, family, school, or social adjustment. While waiting for the appointment date, take time to sit down with a sheet of paper and make up a list of answers to the following questions in areas that may be of concern to you. This can help clarify your thoughts about your child's difficulties. It can also make the evaluation proceed more smoothly and quickly, perhaps even saving time (and money) in the process (professionals usually charge by the quarter hour for their time). Here are the areas to consider:

1. What most concerns you now about your child? Don't go into a long explanation, just list the major problem areas. It helps to identify first of all whether they are mainly problems at home, in school, in the neighborhood or community, or with other children, or in all of these areas. Use these areas as headings on your list. To help a professional help you, it is important that you get down to specifics. What precisely is it that you are concerned about with your child in these areas? Underneath "Home Problems," jot down those problem behaviors that you think are inappropriate for your child's age. That is, these problems seem to occur more often or to a degree that is beyond what you think to be typical of normal children at this age. Even if you do not think they are deviant for your child's age, if you are concerned about them anyway, write them down but indicate this fact next to that item. Now do the same for "School Problems" and the rest of these problem headings (Neighborhood, Peers, and other problem areas). Save this list to take with you to your appointment with the professional.

2. Now on the back of that sheet of paper, or on a new sheet if that one is full, write down these major headings and list anything that comes to mind that your child has difficulties with that might indicate a problem in these areas: Health (chronic or recurring medical problems), Intelligence or Mental Development, Motor Development and Coordination, Problems with Senses (such as eyesight, hearing, etc.), Academic Learning Abilities (such as reading, math, etc.), Anxiety or Fears, Depression, Aggression toward Others, Hyperactivity, Poor Attention, and Antisocial Behavior (such as lying, stealing, setting fires, running away from home, etc.). You may already have listed some of these in #1 above, but it can help to reorganize them into these new categories for your child's professional evaluation.

(cont.)

From *Defiant Children* (2nd ed.): *A Clinician's Manual for Assessment and Parent Training* by Russell A. Barkley. Copyright 1997 by The Guilford Press. Reprinted in *Attention-Deficit Hyperactivity Disorder: A Clinical Workbook* (2nd ed.) by Russell A. Barkley and Kevin R. Murphy. Permission to photocopy this form is granted to purchasers of the *Workbook* for personal use only (see copyright page for details).

3. Some parents may have concerns that they are embarrassed to raise with professionals. These often involve family problems that the parents believe may be contributing to their child's behavioral or emotional problems, but which they are reluctant to divulge to others. Such problems as alcoholism or substance abuse in one of the parents, marital problems that create frequent conflicts between the parents and may spill over into mistreatment of the child, episodes of excessive disciplining or physical punishment that may indicate abuse of the child, and suspected sexual abuse of the child are just some of the many areas parents may be hesitant to divulge to a professional who is a stranger to them. But parents should realize that these are extremely important matters for the mental health professional to understand and take into consideration in attempting to diagnose and treat children. If this information is withheld, then there will be an increased possibility of mistakes in diagnosis, the formulation of the important issues in the case, and treatment planning, because the professional is being intentionally kept in the dark about matters that have a direct bearing on a complete understanding of the case.

4. If at all possible, speak with your child's teacher(s) and write down what they tell you they are most concerned about with your child's school adjustment. Again, save this list to take with you to your child's professional appointment.

5. Now take one more sheet of paper and make a list of any problems you think are occurring in your family besides those of your child. Use the following headings if it will help: *Personal* problems (things you think are troubling you about yourself), *marital* problems, problems with *money*, problems with *relatives*, problems related to your *job* or that of your spouse, problems with *other children* in the family, and *health* problems that you or your spouse may have. Take this list with you to your appointment.

These lists are similar to the areas most likely to be covered in the interview the professional has with you. Keep the lists handy around your home and add items to them as you think of them while waiting for the professional appointment. These lists should help to focus the evaluation quickly on the most important areas of concern that you have about your child and your family. They will also probably help speed up the evaluation and keep things on track. Making these lists probably will help you clarify your own thinking about your current situation and your child's problems. Finally, these lists will help to maximize the usefulness of the evaluation for you and your child. This may result in the professional having greater respect and appreciation for you, a consumer who has come in well prepared for the evaluation.

THE EVALUATION

The clinical interview with you, the parents (and to a lesser extent, with your child), is probably the most important component of a comprehensive professional evaluation of a child. Other important elements are your completed behavior questionnaires about your child, an interview with your child's teacher(s), and similar behavior questionnaires about the child completed by his/her teacher(s).

(cont.)

What Information Will We Need from You to Do the Evaluation?

Plenty! Before professionals can identify or diagnose a child as having behavioral, emotional, or learning problems, they must collect a great deal of information about the child and family, sift through this information looking for the presence of any psychological disorders, determine how serious the problems are likely to be, rule out or rule in other disorders or problems the child might have, and consider what resources are available in your area to deal with these problems. If your child also needs educational or psychological testing for any learning or developmental problems he/she may be having besides the behavior problems, this will be discussed with you on the day of your appointment, and you will be referred to another psychologist or educational specialist for this additional evaluation. You can expect our evaluation to run an average of 2.5–4 hours.

What Else Is Needed to Complete the Evaluation?

Many times our professionals need information from others who know your child, in addition to the information you will give us. You may be asked to (1) give your permission for the professional to get the reports of previous evaluations that your child may have been given; (2) permit the professional to contact your child's treating physician for further information on health status and medication treatment, if any; (3) provide the results of the most recent educational evaluation from your child's school; (4) initiate one of these school evaluations, if one was not already done and if one of your concerns is your child's school adjustment; (5) complete the packet of behavior questionnaires about your child that should have been sent to you earlier by mail; (6) return these forms before the appointment date; (7) give your permission to have your child's teacher(s) complete similar behavior questionnaires, which will be mailed to them; and (8) give permission for the professional to obtain any information from social service agencies that already may be involved in providing services to your child.

There is rarely any reason for you to deny our professionals your permission to obtain the above information from others or for you to refuse to institute the procedures requested of you. However, on rare occasions, you may wish an unbiased second opinion about your child's problems. This may happen if you have already had an evaluation by the school or another professional with which you strongly disagree. In such cases, you may wish to tell us not to obtain the records from the other professional or from any school evaluation. Should you do so, please explain why you are withholding your permission for the release of these particular sources of information so that we have a clearer grasp of the issues involved in your request for this new evaluation with us. However, in most cases you should not deny our professionals access to the information that can be provided by your child's teachers, even if you disagree with those teachers. Preventing professionals from speaking with your child's teachers greatly diminishes the ability of those professionals to understand your child. It precludes their getting information from the second most important caregiver in your child's current situation. If you disagree with what a teacher may say, explain this to the professionals before they contact the school so they can keep this disagreement in mind as they speak with the teacher.

(cont.)

What Happens on the Day of the Appointment?

Several things. You are going to be interviewed for about 1–2 hours about your child, and your child most likely will be interviewed as well. It is the interview with you that is most important. You probably are going to be asked to complete some behavior questionnaires as well, if you were not sent any to complete before the appointment. Your child may also be tested if there are issues to be answered about his/her intelligence, language and academic skills, or other mental abilities (such as memory, motor skills, etc.).

The Parent Interview

The interview with you, the parent, is an indispensable part of the evaluation of your child. No adult is more likely to have the wealth of knowledge about, the history of interactions with, or simply the time spent with a child than you. Whenever possible, both parents should attend the interview, as they each have a somewhat unique perspective on the child's problems. If employment or other reasons preclude one parent from attending, the other parent should speak with the partner the day before the evaluation and write down that parent's concerns and opinions about the child to take into the evaluation the next day. It is usually not necessary that brothers and sisters attend this first evaluation. In some cases, the professional may request that these siblings attend a second meeting if the professional feels it is necessary to get the siblings' view of particular family conflicts or problems the siblings are having with the child being evaluated.

The interview with you serves several purposes. First, it establishes an important relationship between you and the professional and even between the child and the professional, which will be helpful and put you at ease with the rest of the evaluation. Second, the interview provides an important source of invaluable information about your child and family. In particular, it gives the professional your view of your child's apparent problems and narrows the focus of later stages of the evaluation. This is your chance to get your concerns about your child out in the open with a knowledgeable professional. Don't be shy, coy, or unforthcoming. The more information you can provide the professional, the better appreciation he/she can have of your child's problems and the more accurate the diagnosis is likely to be. Use the lists that you constructed while waiting for the appointment date so you don't forget anything you wanted to discuss. Third, the interview can often reveal just how much distress the child's problems are causing you and your family. It also gives the professional some sense of your own well-being as a parent. Fourth, the interview may begin to reveal significant information about your relationship with your child that could be important in pinpointing some potential contributors to your child's problem. But two of the most important purposes of this evaluation are to determine a diagnosis of your child's problem(s) and to provide you with reasonable treatment recommendations.

The professional is likely to make notes throughout the conversation with you. He/she will also jot down his/her own observations of you and how your child is doing while you both are in the clinic. Although these notes from observing you and your child may be helpful in raising certain ideas about your child's problems that can be discussed with you later, they will not be overly emphasized by our professionals. Behavior in the office, particular that of your child, is often not

(cont.)

very helpful in telling us how your child is likely to behave at home or in school. In general, research with children having behavior problems has shown that many are likely to behave normally during this evaluation. Such normal behavior will not be interpreted by our professionals as indicating that your child has no problems. However, if your child displays a lot of inattentive, hyperactive, or defiant behavior during the evaluation, this may be more informative, as such behavior is unusual for normal children and could indicate your child would have similar problems in school.

Some of our professionals like to have your child present during the interview with you. In part, this is to give them some idea of how you and your child get along with each other. This is fine so long as your child is not likely to be upset by the nature of the questions and with your answers about your child. Some parents do not feel comfortable with this situation as they do not want to talk about the child's problems in front of him/her, at least not yet. If you feel that having your child present during the interview would make you inhibited and less candid about your opinions and concerns, then simply advise the professionals politely of your feelings on the matter when you first meet with them the day of the evaluation. It should not be a problem for us to handle things your way.

INFORMATION ABOUT YOUR CHILD

The interview will probably begin with an explanation of the procedures to be undertaken as part of this evaluation and the time it is expected to take. If it has not been discussed already, the estimated cost of the evaluation and the manner in which the fee is to be handled (e.g., insurance, self-pay, etc.) should be discussed with you. Our professionals may point out to you at this time that although most of what you say is confidential (they cannot tell anyone else about what you have said without your permission), laws may place limits on this privilege. These limits are about reports of child neglect or abuse. Where you mention such information to the professional, he/she may be required by law to report this information to the state, usually the Department of Social Services. The clinician will tell you about such limits on the day of your evaluation.

The interview will probably proceed to a discussion of your concerns about your child. You can refer to the notes that you made before the appointment here. You will probably be asked to give some specific examples of your child's behavior that illustrate why you are concerned about it. For instance, if you say that you are worried that your child is too impulsive, you may be asked to give some examples of your child's impulsive behavior. This is done not to challenge your opinion but to help the interviewer see how you arrived at that opinion. Give as much information as you can when asked. You may also be asked how you are presently trying to manage your child's behavior problems and whether your spouse is using a different approach. It is common for behavior problem children to be somewhat better behaved for their fathers than mothers. It is all right to describe such differences as they do not mean you or your spouse are doing anything wrong or are causing the problems with your child.

You are going to be questioned about when you first noticed your child's problems and how long each of the major problem areas has been occurring. Try to be as specific as your memory will permit. Again, taking some notes about this before the appointment may help you to remember

(cont.)

this information better when you are asked. This naturally leads to questions about the types of previous professional assistance you may have obtained and whether it is possible for the interviewer to contact these other professionals for further details about your child and your family. Our professionals like to ask parents what they believe has led their child to develop these problems. If you have an opinion on what caused your child's problems, it is all right to say it, but don't be afraid simply to say you don't know. The professional is just looking to see if you can provide him/her with any additional insight about the cause of your child's difficulties. Remember, we as professionals do not know the exact causes of all children's behavior problems, although we have much information that can be of help to us in narrowing down these possibilities. Sometimes it simply is not possible to say for sure why certain children behave the way they do. Don't feel as though you have to come up with a better explanation for your child's behavior.

If you completed behavior rating forms before the appointment and returned them, the professional may want to review some of your answers with you now, especially those that may have been unclear to him/her. If the professional does not go over your answers with you, *you* may want to ask *the professional* if he/she has any questions about your answers on those forms. You may also be asked about some answers on the forms that were sent to your child's teacher(s). If you are curious, you may ask to see the teacher's answers on these forms. It is your right to see what the teacher has said. Ask the professional to explain anything about these forms and their answers that is confusing to you.

The professional will also talk with you about any problems your child has within a number of different developmental domains. We customarily ask parents about their children's development so far in their physical health, sensory and motor abilities, language, thinking, intellect, academic achievement, self-help skills such as dressing and bathing, social behavior, emotional problems, and family relationships. You will probably be asked about similar things. Many professionals will also review with you a variety of behavior problems or symptoms of other psychiatric problems to see if your child also may be having these difficulties. Simply be truthful and indicate whether or not these other symptoms are present and to what degree.

Because our professionals are trying to evaluate your child's problems, they are likely to spend most or all of the time with you trying to identify the areas of concern you have about your child. This is fine. But our professionals also want to ask you about any strengths your child has in any of the areas discussed above or in particular hobbies, sports, or school subjects. If the professional does not ask you, then mention some yourself to give a more complete and balanced picture of your child to the professional. We also like to take an opportunity to ask parents about possible special interests, privileges, and rewards that your child enjoys. We can typically use this information later if we have to set up a reward program for your child as part of our behavior management training with parents.

At some point in the interview, the professional may review your child's developmental and medical history with you. You will have completed a form about this for us before the appointment, but we may want to review your answers with you as part of the interview.

(cont.)

31

It is essential that the professional discuss with you your child's school history. Many children referred to us have difficulties adjusting to the demands of school. You are likely to be asked about the age at which your child began kindergarten, what school he/she attended, and how well your child progressed through this and subsequent grades and schools. You probably will be questioned about the types of special educational evaluations and placements your child has received, if any, and whether your child had a team evaluation conducted by the school. If one has not been done, you may be asked to initiate one in case your child has school problems that make the child eligible for any formal special educational services. You are also going to be asked about what specific concerns your child's teacher(s) have raised about school performance, both now and in the past. Be sure to tell the professional if your child has repeated a grade, or has been suspended or expelled. We also like to question parents about the nature of the relationship they presently have with the school staff working with their child. Is it friendly and supportive, or filled with conflict? Has communication been open and reasonably clear, or limited and hostile? This greatly helps us in preparing for later contacts with the school staff if these are needed. If the professional forgets to ask about this, you may want to raise the topic yourself to give the professional a clearer picture of your past relations with the school staff.

You may be asked to give written permission for the professional to contact your child's school, if it was not obtained previously from you. You should consent to this under most circumstances, as it is very hard for a professional to evaluate your child's problems fully without access to the school's information. If you do not want this done, be sure to give the professionals a clear explanation as to why you do not, so they do not misjudge you as being unreasonably hostile to them or to the school.

INFORMATION ABOUT YOU AND YOUR FAMILY

Professionals know that many families of behavior problem children are under more stress than other families and that the parents may be having more personal problems than most parents whose children do not have behavior problems. Do not be offended if you are asked such personal questions. Information about you and your family can be of great assistance to the professional in helping to understand your child's problems better and develop more useful treatment recommendations for you. It may also indicate to the interviewer that you may need some additional help for your own or your family's other problems. You will probably be asked about your own background, education, and occupation, as well as those of your spouse. The professional may ask if you or your spouse have had any psychiatric, learning, developmental, or chronic medical problems. Parents are also typically asked during such evaluations whether they are having marital problems and what the nature of these might be. All of these personal questions are routine and important, so please answer as honestly as you can.

We will ask you about other children in the immediate family and any psychological, educational, developmental, or other problems these siblings may be having.

Before the interview with you is over, take a minute to review the notes that you brought with you to see if all of your concerns have been covered with the professional you are seeing. Share with

(cont.)

the professional any further information on these notes or anything else you feel might be helpful in better understanding your child and your family. Your candor and openness will be respected and appreciated by our professional staff.

The Child Interview

Depending on your child's age and intelligence, some time during the evaluation will be spent by the professional in interviewing your child and making some informal observations of your child's appearance, behavior, and developmental skills. This interview serves much the same purposes as the interview with you. However, you should not place too much emphasis on the information we obtain in this interview. Such informal observations of your child's conduct during the interview may not be typical of your child's behavior at home or school, as mentioned earlier. Our professionals will not make the mistake of placing too much weight on the observations of your child in our clinic. Do not be surprised to find that your child is well behaved during this evaluation, and do not worry about it.

Your child is probably going to be asked a lot of general questions. These will probably deal with the following areas:

1. What is your child's awareness of why he/she is visiting the interviewer today and what have the parents told him/her about the reason for the visit?
2. What are the child's favorite hobbies, television shows, sports, or pets?
3. Where does the child attend school, who are his/her teachers, what types of subjects does he/she take in school, and which does he/she like most? If the child is doing poorly in a subject, what reasons does he/she give to explain any such difficulties?
4. Does the child see him/herself as having any behavior problems in the classroom? What types of discipline does the child get from the teacher(s) for any such misconduct?
5. How does the child think he/she is accepted by other children at school?
6. What are your child's perceptions of any of the problems that you have reported to the professional?
7. What would your child like to see changed or improved at home or at school?
8. The professional may then ask your child about whether he/she sees him/herself as having any behavioral problems. If the child does, he/she will likely be asked why and what he/she thinks causes this pattern of behavior.

Our professionals are aware that children are notorious for underreporting their difficulties and are likely to do so in this part of the interview. Thus, the professional will not use your child's answers in determining if the child actually has a behavioral, learning, or emotional disorder.

Some of our professionals find it helpful during this interview, particularly if it is with young children, to let them play, draw, or simply wander about the office. Others may ask them a series of incomplete sentences, letting the children fill in the blanks with their own answers. This can be a less direct way of finding out children's feelings about themselves and other features of their lives.

(cont.)

The Teacher Interview

Although it is not necessarily conducted on the same day, the teacher interview is an essential part of your child's evaluation. Next to parents, few other adults will have spent more time with your child than his/her teachers, particularly if the child is of elementary school age. The opinions the teachers hold of the children are a critical part of the evaluation of any child and will be obtained by our professionals in most cases. In all but the most unusual circumstances, you should consent to this exchange of information, as it is in the best interest of your child's evaluation. This interview will likely be done by telephone.

The teachers most likely will be questioned about your child's current academic and behavioral problems. Relations with classmates also may be covered during this discussion. How your child acts in various school situations, especially where work has to be done, will likely be covered. We also like to ask teachers about situations that involve limited or no supervision, such as during recess, lunch, or special assemblies; while in hallways or bathrooms; or on the bus. The professional should also find out what the teachers are currently doing to manage the child's problems. Your child's performance in each academic subject should be briefly discussed. The professional may ask if your child has received a multidisciplinary team evaluation as part of the child's rights under state laws. If not, the professional may question the teacher as to whether one should be initiated in case special educational resources are going to be needed to help your child.

SUMMARY

Interviews with you and your child and contact with your child's teachers form an indispensable part of our evaluation of your child. These interviews provide a wealth of information useful to making a diagnosis and planning treatments for your child that simply cannot be obtained by any other means. Throughout these interviews, sufficient time must be taken by the professional to explore the necessary topics with each person to obtain as thorough a picture of your child as needed. A 20-minute initial interview will simply not suffice! The average length of time devoted to interviewing alone is often 1–2 hours, not including any psychological testing of the child. It will also be important for the professional to obtain parent and teacher behavior rating scales of your child's behavior. Some children will also require academic or psychological testing to rule out other developmental or learning disabilities, but these will not be done on the day of your evaluation. If they are needed, you will be told by your professional as to why testing is needed and where it can be obtained.

We hope you have found this pamphlet useful in preparing for your child's evaluation with our professional staff.

CLINICAL INTERVIEW—PARENT REPORT FORM

Child's name_____ **Informant**_____

Informant's relationship to child: [*Circle one*]   Mother   Father   Other:_____

Record/chart #_____ Interviewer_____ Date_____

Child's date of birth_____ Age: Years_____ Months_____

Referral source_____ (e.g., school, physician, etc.)

Does referring person wish a copy of the report from this evaluation?   Yes   No

Clinical Diagnoses: [*To be filled in after evaluation is completed*]

1._____ 2._____ 3._____

Clinical Recommendations: [*To be briefly listed after evaluation is completed*]

1. _____
2. _____
3. _____
4. _____
5. _____
6. _____
7. _____
8. _____
9. _____
10. _____

LEGAL DISCLOSURES

[*Interviewer: At the start of the interview, be certain to review any necessary legal disclosures pertinent to your state, county, or other geographic region. For instance, in Massachusetts, we advise parents of the following four issues:*

1. *Any disclosure of information that indicates a suspicion of child abuse must be reported to state authorities (Department of Social Services).*

(*cont.*)

From *Defiant Children* (2nd ed.): *A Clinician's Manual for Assessment and Parent Training* by Russell A. Barkley. Copyright 1997 by The Guilford Press. Reprinted in *Attention-Deficit Hyperactivity Disorder: A Clinical Workbook* (2nd ed.) by Russell A. Barkley and Kevin R. Murphy. Permission to photocopy this form is granted to purchasers of the *Workbook* for personal use only (see copyright page for details).

2. *Any disclosure of threats of harm to oneself, as in a specific suicide threat, will result in immediate referral to an emergency mental health unit.*
3. *Any disclosure of specific threats to specific individuals will result in notification of those individuals concerning the threat.*
4. *Although the mental health records are confidential, they may be subpoenaed by a judge's order and must be provided to the court if so ordered.*

Take time now to cover any such issues with the family before proceeding to the remainder of this interview.]

FAMILY COMPOSITION

Is this child: _____Your biological child _____Adopted _____Foster child

With which parent does the child live? _____Both _____Mother only _____Father only

_____Neither parent; child lives with _____Grandparent _____In foster care

Do you have legal custody of this child?   Yes   No   [*Interviewer: If No, determine whether or not it is legally advisable or permissible to proceed with this evaluation.*]

Does any other adult live in the home?   Yes   No   If so, who is it?_____

How many children are in the family?_____ How many are still at home?_____

PARENTAL CONCERNS ABOUT CHILD—REASONS FOR EVALUATION

What are you most concerned about regarding your child that led you to request this evaluation? [*Organize parent's responses under major headings below. Query parents about (1) the specific details of each concern, (2) when it began, (3) how often it occurs or how severe it is, and (4) what they have tried to do so far to deal with it.*]

Home behavior management problems:

Home emotional reaction problems:

(cont.)

Developmental delays: [*If present, consider reviewing with parents the diagnostic criteria for Mental Retardation or other specific developmental disorders such as learning disorders.*]

School behavior management problems:

School work performance or learning problems:

School emotional reaction problems:

Social interaction problems with peers:

Behavior in the community (outside of home and school):

Other concerns:

Why have you decided to seek this evaluation of your child at this time?

(cont.)

What type of assistance or treatment recommendations do you hope to receive from this evaluation?

Now that you have told me what your main concerns about your child are that bring you here today and what you hope to gain from the evaluation, I need to go over a number of different topics with you about your child. This needs to be done to be sure that I get as comprehensive a picture of your child's psychological adjustment as possible. I am going to ask you about a number of important developmental areas for any child. You should tell me if you have noticed anything unusual, abnormal, atypical, or even bizarre about your child's functioning in any of these areas. Let's begin with your child's:

Sensory development (impairments in vision, hearing, sense of touch or smell; abnormal reactions to sensory stimulation; hallucinations, etc.):

Motor development (coordination, gait, balance, posture, movements, gestures, tics, nervous habits or mannerisms, etc.):

Language development (delays, comprehension problems, speech difficulties):

Emotional development (overreactions, mood swings, extreme or unpredictable moods, peculiar or odd emotions, unusual fears or anxieties, etc.):

Thinking (odd ideas, bizarre preoccupations or fixations, unusual fantasies, speaks in incomplete or incoherent thoughts, delusions):

(cont.)

Social behavior (aggressive, rejected, bullies others, withdrawn, shy, anxious around others, mute when with others, aloof from others or shows no desire for friends/playmates, etc.):

Intelligence/academic skills (delays in general mental development; problems with memory; or specific delays in reading, math, spelling, handwriting, or other academic skill areas):

REVIEW OF DSM-IV CHILDHOOD DISORDERS

Now I need to ask you about a number of very specific questions about a variety of behavioral, social, or emotional problems that children sometimes have difficulties with. As I ask you about these things, keep in mind that some of these things are not bad or abnormal and may be seen sometimes in healthy, normal children. I want you to tell me if your child does any of these things to a degree that you consider to be inappropriate for someone of his/her age and sex.

[*Interviewer: If this child is a member of a minority group in this country or used to reside in a foreign country, be sure to follow up any answer by the parent that endorses a symptom as present with the following question: "Yes, but do you consider this to be a problem or to be inappropriate for a child of your ethnic or cultural group?"*]

Oppositional Defiant Disorder

[*Interviewer: Diagnosis requires four or more symptoms. Symptoms must be inappropriate for child's age; have lasted at least the past 6 months; and must be producing clear evidence of clinically significant impairment in social, academic, or occupational functioning.*]

I am now going to ask you some specific questions about your child's behavior during the past 6 months. For each of the behaviors I ask you about, please tell me if your child shows that behavior to a degree that is inappropriate compared to other children of your child's age.

A. Oppositional Defiant List [*Enter 1 if present, 0 if absent, and ? if unknown.*]

   During the past 6 months, did your child show any of the following:

   1. Often loses temper ———
   2. Often argues with adults ———

(cont.)

Note. The questions in the remainder of this form are adapted from the diagnostic criteria of the DSM-IV (American Psychiatric Association, 1994). Copyright 1994 by the American Psychiatric Association. Adapted by permission.

3. Often actively defies or refuses to comply with adults' requests or rules ____
4. Often deliberately annoys people ____
5. Often blames others for his/her own mistakes or misbehavior ____
6. Is often touchy or easily annoyed by others ____
7. Is often angry or resentful ____
8. Is often spiteful or vindictive ____

B. Have these behaviors existed for at least the past 6 months? [*Enter 1 if present, 0 if absent, and ? if unknown.*] ____

C. At what age did these behaviors first cause problems for your child? ____ (yrs.)

D. Have these behaviors created problems or impairment for your child in either of the following areas? [*Enter 1 if present, 0 if absent, and ? if unknown.*]
Social relations with others ____ Academic performance ____

E. Exclusion Criteria: [*Interviewer: Enter 1 if symptoms occur only during a Psychotic Disorder or Mood Disorder or if criteria are met for Conduct Disorder. Enter 0 if not, ? if unknown.*] ____

Diagnostic Code

Requirements for diagnosis:

Does section A total 4 or more? ____
Does section B total 1? ____
Does section D total 1 or more? ____
Does section E total 0? ____

[*Check here if all requirements are met.*]
☐ ODD (313.81)

Conduct Disorder

[*Interviewer: Diagnosis requires three or more symptoms during previous 12 months and at least one during the past 6 months; the symptoms must presently be causing impairment in social or academic functioning.*]

Now I want to ask you about some other things your child may have done. For these behaviors, I want you to think about the past 12 months and tell me whether any of these have occurred during that time.

A. Conduct Disorder List [*Enter 1 if present, 0 if absent, and ? if unknown.*]
During the past 12 months, did your child do any of the following:

1. Often bullies, threatens, or intimidates others ____
2. Often initiates physical fights ____

(cont.)

3. Has used a weapon that can cause serious physical harm to others (e.g., a bat, brick, broken bottle, knife, or gun)   ____
4. Has been physically cruel to people   ____
5. Has been physically cruel to animals   ____
6. Has stolen while confronting a victim (e.g., mugging, purse snatching, extortion, armed robbery)   ____
7. Has forced someone into sexual activity   ____
8. Has deliberately engaged in fire setting with the intention of causing serious damage   ____
9. Has deliberately destroyed others' property (other than by fire setting)   ____
10. Has broken into someone else's house, building, or car   ____
11. Often lies to obtain goods or favors or to avoid obligations (i.e., "cons" others)   ____
12. Has stolen items of nontrivial value without confronting a victim (e.g., shoplifting, but without breaking and entering; forgery)   ____
13. Often stays out at night despite parental prohibitions   ____
    If so, at what age did this begin? ____ (yrs.)
    [Interviewer: Must begin before age 13 years to be counted as a symptom.]
14. Has run away from home overnight at least twice while living in parent's home, foster care, or group home   ____
    If so, how many times?   ____
    [Interviewer: Count as a symptom if it occurred once without child returning for a lengthy period.]
15. Is often truant from school   ____
    If so, at what age did he/she begin doing this? ____ (yrs.)
    [Interviewer: Must begin before age 13 years to be counted as a symptom.]

B. Have three of these behaviors occurred during the past 12 months? [Enter 1 if present, 0 if absent, and ? if unknown.]   ____

C. Has at least one of these behaviors occurred during the past 6 months? [Enter 1 if present, 0 if absent, and ? if unknown.]   ____

D. Did any of these behaviors occur prior to age 10 years? [Enter 1 if present, 0 if absent, and ? if unknown.]   ____

E. Have these behaviors created problems or impairment for your child in either of the following areas? [Enter 1 if present, 0 if absent, and ? if unknown.]
   Social relations with others ____ Academic performance ____

F. Exclusion Criteria: [Interviewer: Enter 1 if the child is 18 years of age or older and criteria are met for Antisocial Personality Disorder. Enter 0 if not, ? if unknown.]   ____

(cont.)

Diagnostic Code

Requirements for diagnosis:

Does section A total 3 or more? _____
Does section B total 1? _____
Does section C total 1? _____
Does section E total 1 or more? _____
Does section F total 0? _____

[*Check one subtype if all requirements are met.*]

☐ CD, Childhood-Onset Type (312.8) [*Onset of at least one symptom prior to age 10 years*]
☐ CD, Adolescent-Onset Type (312.8) [*Absence of any symptoms prior to age 10 years*]

Severity: [*Check appropriate severity level*]

☐ Mild [*Few, if any, conduct problems in excess of those required to make the diagnosis and conduct problems cause only minor harm to others.*]
☐ Moderate [*Number of conduct problems and effect on others is intermediate between "mild" and "severe."*]
☐ Severe [*Many conduct problems have occurred in excess of those required to make the diagnosis or conduct problems cause considerable harm to others.*]

Disruptive Behavior Disorder, NOS

[*Interviewer: This category is for disruptive disorders characterized by conduct or oppositional defiant behaviors that do not meet criteria for CD or ODD but that produce clinically significant impairment.*]

Disruptive Behavior Disorder, NOS (312.9)

Attention-Deficit/Hyperactivity Disorder

[*Interviewer: Diagnosis requires six Inattention symptoms and/or six Hyperactive–Impulsive symptoms. Symptoms must also be inappropriate for child's age, have lasted at least the past 6 months, and have caused some impairment prior to age 7 years; presently must be causing impairment in two situations (home, school, or work functioning); and must be producing clear evidence of clinically significant impairment in social or academic functioning.*]

Let me ask you about some other behaviors that your child may have shown during the past 6 months. Again, for each of the behaviors I ask you about, please tell me if your child shows that behavior to a degree that is inappropriate compared to other children of your child's age.

A. Inattention List [*Enter 1 if present, 0 if absent, and ? if unknown.*]

During the past 6 months, did your child show any of the following:

1. Often fails to give close attention to details or makes careless mistakes in schoolwork, work, or other activities _____

(cont.)

2. Often has difficulty sustaining attention in tasks or play activities ____

3. Often does not seem to listen when spoken to directly ____

4. Often does not follow through on instructions and fails to finish schoolwork, chores, or duties at work [*Interviewer: Inquire to be sure this is not due solely to oppositional behavior or failure to understand instructions.*] ____

5. Often has difficulty organizing tasks and activities ____

6. Often avoids, dislikes, or is reluctant to engage in tasks that require sustained mental effort (such as schoolwork or homework) ____

7. Often loses things necessary for tasks or activities (e.g., toys, school assignments, pencils, books, or tools) ____

8. Is often easily distracted by extraneous stimuli ____

9. Is often forgetful in daily activities ____

B. Hyperactive–Impulsive List [*Enter 1 if present, 0 if absent, and ? if unknown.*]

During the past 6 months, did your child show any of the following:

1. Often fidgets with hands or feet or squirms in his/her seat ____

2. Often leaves his/her seat in the classroom or in other situations in which remaining seated is expected ____

3. Often runs about or climbs excessively in situations in which it is inappropriate to do so [*Interviewer: For adolescents, this may be limited to subjective feelings of restlessness.*] ____

4. Often has difficulty playing or engaging in leisure activities quietly ____

5. Is often "on the go" or often acts as if "driven by a motor" ____

6. Often talks excessively ____

7. Often blurts out answers before questions have been completed ____

8. Often has difficulty awaiting his/her turn ____

9. Often interrupts or intrudes on others (e.g., butts into conversations or games) ____

C. Have these behaviors existed for at least the past 6 months? [*Enter 1 if present, 0 if absent, and ? if unknown.*] ____

D. At what age did these behaviors first cause problems for your child? [*Interviewer: Onset by age 13 is acceptable, although DSM-IV stipulates age 7.*] ____ (yrs.)

E. During the past 6 months, have these behaviors caused problems for this child in any of these situations? [*Enter 1 if present, 0 if absent, and ? if unknown.*]

At home ____ In school ____ At daycare or babysitters ____

In community activities (clubs, sports, scouts, etc.) ____

F. Have these behaviors created problems or impairment for your child in any of the following areas? [*Enter 1 if present, 0 if absent, and ? if unknown.*]

Social relations with others ____ Academic performance ____

(cont.)

G. Exclusion Criteria: [*Interviewer: Enter 1 if symptoms occur only during
a Pervasive Developmental Disorder or Psychotic Disorder or are better accounted
for by another mental disorder, such as a Mood, Anxiety, Dissociative, or
Personality Disorder. Enter 0 if not, ? if unknown.*]   ____

Diagnostic Code

Requirements for diagnosis:

Does section A total 6 or more, or does section B total 6 or more? ____
Does section C total 1? ____
Does section E total 2 or more? ____
Does section F total 1 or more? ____
Does section G total 0? ____

[*Check one subtype if all requirements are met.*]

☐ ADHD, Combined Type (314.01) [*Meets criteria for both Inattention and Hyperactive–
Impulsive lists*]
☐ ADHD, Predominantly Inattentive Type (314.00) [*Meets criteria only for Inattention items*]
☐ ADHD, Predominantly Hyperactive–Impulsive Type (314.01) [*Meets criteria only for
Hyperactive–Impulsive items*]
☐ ADHD, NOS (Not Otherwise Specified) (314.9) [*For disorders with prominent symptoms
that do not meet full criteria for any subtype of ADHD*]

For individuals (especially adolescents and adults) who currently have symptoms that no longer
meet full criteria, specify "In Partial Remission": _____

ANXIETY AND MOOD DISORDERS

Now I would like to ask you some questions about your child's emotions in general and his/her
emotional reactions to some specific situations. I'll begin by asking you about any specific fears
that your child may have. Then I will ask you about his/her general mood or emotional condition
throughout much of the day. Let's start with some specific fears that your child may have.

Specific Phobia

[*Interviewer: Diagnosis requires that each criteria A–F below be met.*]

A. Does your child show a marked and persistent fear that is excessive or unreasonable
in response to the presence of or the anticipation of a specific object or situation?
For instance, in response to or anticipation of certain animals, heights, being in the
dark, thunderstorms or lightning, flying, receiving an injection, seeing blood, or any
other things or situations? [*Enter 1 if present, 0 if absent, and ? if unknown.*]   ____

(*cont.*)

[*Interviewer: If A is present, answer the following then proceed to B–G below; otherwise, skip to the next disorder. If any of criteria B–F are not met, skip to the next disorder.*]

What specifically is your child fearful of? _____

B. Does your child have this anxious or fearful reaction almost invariably when exposed to (specific thing or situation)? [*Enter 1 if present, 0 if absent, and ? if unknown.*] ____

[*Interviewer: This may include a panic attack in the presence of the feared object or situation; or anxiety expressed by crying, tantrums, freezing, or clinging. Also, children do not need to recognize that their fear is excessive or unreasonable to qualify for this diagnosis.*]

C. Does your child attempt to avoid this thing or situation, or, if he/she must be exposed to it, does he/she endure it with intense anxiety or distress? [*Enter 1 if present, 0 if absent, and ? if unknown.*] ____

D. Does your child's avoidance of, anticipation of, or anxious reaction to this thing or situation interfere significantly with any of the following? [*Enter 1 if present, 0 if absent, and ? if unknown.*]

[*Interviewer: Only one of these conditions needs to be endorsed for this criterion to be met.*]

His/her normal routine ____ Academic functioning ____

Social activities ____ Social relationships ____

E. Does having this fear cause him/her marked distress? ____

F. Has your child had this fearful or anxious reaction to this thing or event over a period of at least the past 6 months? [*Enter 1 if present, 0 if absent, and ? if unknown.*] ____

G. Exclusion Criteria: [*Interviewer: Enter 1 if this phobia or anxiety is better accounted for by another mental disorder, such as Obsessive–Compulsive Disorder, Posttraumatic Stress Disorder, Separation Anxiety Disorder, Social Phobia, or Panic Disorder. Enter 0 if not, ? if unknown.*] ____

Diagnostic Code

Requirements for diagnosis:

Does each section A through E equal 1 or more? ____
Does section F total 0? ____

[*Check here if all requirements are met.*]

☐ Specific Phobia (300.29)

Social Phobia

[*Interviewer: Diagnosis requires that each criteria A–F below be met, but the child must have developed the capacity for age-appropriate social relationships with familiar people and the anxiety must occur in peer settings, not just in interactions with adults.*]

(cont.)

What about social situations?

A. [*Enter 1 if present, 0 if absent, and ? if unknown.*]

   1. Does your child show a marked and persistent fear that is excessive or unreasonable in response to the presence of or the anticipation of a social or performance situation in which he/she is exposed to unfamiliar people or to possible scrutiny by others? ____

   2. Does your child fear that he/she will act in a way that will be embarrassing or humiliating or will be so anxious that it will be humiliating or embarrassing for him/her? ____

   [*Interviewer: If parts 1 and 2 of A are present, answer the next question and then proceed with remaining criteria below; otherwise, skip to the next disorder. If any of the remaining criteria below are not met, skip to the next disorder.*]

   3. What specific social situation is your child fearful of? _____

B. Does your child have this anxious or fearful reaction almost invariably when exposed to this situation? [*Enter 1 if present, 0 if absent, and ? if unknown.*] ____

   [*Interviewer: This may include a panic attack in this social situation or anxiety expressed by crying, tantrums, freezing, clinging, or shrinking from this social situation with unfamiliar people. Also, children do not need to recognize that their fear is excessive or unreasonable to qualify for this diagnosis.*]

C. Does your child attempt to avoid this situation or, if he/she must be exposed to it, does he/she endure it with intense anxiety or distress? [*Enter 1 if present, 0 if absent, and ? if unknown.*] ____

D. Does your child's avoidance of, anticipation of, or anxious reaction to this situation interfere significantly with any of the following? [*Enter 1 if present, 0 if absent, and ? if unknown.*]

   [*Interviewer: Only one of these conditions needs to be endorsed for this criterion to be met.*]

   His/her normal routine ____ Academic functioning ____

   Social activities ____ Social relationships ____

E. Does having this fear cause him/her marked distress? ____

F. Has your child had this fearful or anxious reaction to this situation for at least the past 6 months? [*Enter 1 if present, 0 if absent, and ? if unknown.*] ____

G. Exclusion Criteria: [*Interviewer: Enter 1 if this phobia or anxiety is due to the direct physiological effects of a substance or a general medical condition, or is not better accounted for by another mental disorder, such as Panic Disorder, Separation Anxiety Disorder, Body Dysmorphic Disorder, Pervasive Developmental Disorder, or Schizoid Personality Disorder. Or, if a general medical condition or another mental disorder is present, enter 1 if the fear in Criterion A above is related to it. Enter 0 if not, ? if unknown.*] ____

(cont.)

Diagnostic Code

Requirements for diagnosis:

Does section A total 2? _____
Does each section B through F equal 1 or more? _____
Does section G total 0? _____

[*Check here if all requirements are met.*]

☐ Social Phobia (300.23)
Specify if Generalized (fear includes most social situations): _____

Separation Anxiety Disorder

[*Interviewer: Diagnosis requires that at least three symptoms be present (see A below) for at least 4 weeks. The symptoms must have developed before age 18 years and must produce clinically significant distress or impairment in social, academic, or other important areas of functioning, and other disorders must be excluded as indicated below.*]

A. Separation Anxiety Disorder Symptom List

Now let's talk about how your child reacts emotionally when he/she must be away from you or when he/she must leave home for activities in the community. Does your child show any of the following? [*Enter 1 if present, 0 if absent, and ? if unknown.*]

1. Recurrent, excessive distress when separation from home, or from a parent or major attachment figures, occurs or is anticipated _____

2. Persistent and excessive worry about losing a parent or major attachment figure or about possible harm occurring to such a figure _____

3. Persistent and excessive worry that an unexpected or untoward event will lead him/her to become separated from a parent or major attachment figure (e.g., getting lost or being kidnapped) _____

4. Persistent reluctance or refusal to go to school or elsewhere because of fear of separation _____

5. Persistent and excessive fear or reluctance to be alone, or without a parent or major attachment figure at home, or without such a parent or caregiver when in other settings _____

6. Persistent reluctance or refusal to go to sleep without being near a major attachment figure or to sleep away from home _____

7. Repeated nightmares involving the theme or topic of separation from a parent or other caregiver _____

8. Repeated complaints of physical symptoms, such as headaches, stomachaches, nausea, or vomiting, when separation from a parent or major attachment figure occurs or is anticipated _____

[*Interviewer: If three or more symptoms were endorsed, proceed with remaining criteria; otherwise, skip to next disorder. If any of the remaining criteria below are not met, skip to the next disorder.*]

(cont.)

B. Have these fears existed for at least 4 weeks? [*Enter 1 if present, 0 if absent, and ?* *if unknown.*]   ____

C. At what age did these behaviors first cause problems for your child? ____ (yrs.)

[*Interviewer: Symptoms must have developed before age 18 years.*]

D. Have these worries created distress for your child or impairment in any of the following areas? [*Enter 1 if present, 0 if absent, and ? if unknown.*]

Social relations with others ____ Academic performance ____

Any other areas of functioning ____

E. Exclusion Criteria: [*Interviewer: Enter 1 if symptoms occur only during a Pervasive Developmental Disorder, Schizophrenia, or other Psychotic Disorder, or are not better accounted for by Panic Disorder. Enter 0 if not, ? if unknown.*]   ____

Diagnostic Code

Requirements for diagnosis:

Does section A total 3 or more? ____
Does section B total 1? ____
Does section C show 17 years or less? ____
Does section D total 1 or more? ____
Does section E total 0? ____

[*Check here if all requirements are met.*]

☐ Separation Anxiety Disorder (309.21)
Specify if Early Onset (before age 6 years): _____

Generalized Anxiety Disorder

[*Interviewer: Diagnosis requires that criteria A and B be met; at least one symptom in criterion C be present for at least 6 months on more days than not; that symptoms produce clinically significant distress or impairment in social, academic, or other important areas of functioning; and that other disorders be excluded as indicated below.*]

Now let's talk about whether your child tends to be generally anxious or to worry a lot compared to other children of his/her age group.

A. [*Enter 1 if present, 0 if absent, and ? if unknown.*]

1. Does your child show excessive anxiety and worry about a number of events or activities, such as work activities, school performance, or any other situations? ____

2. Has this anxiety or worry occurred on more days than not for at least the last 6 months? ____

(*cont.*)

[Interviewer: If the questions in A above were endorsed, proceed with remaining criteria for this disorder; otherwise, skip to next disorder. If any of the remaining criteria below are not met, skip to the next disorder.]

B. Does your child find it difficult to control his/her worry? ____

C. Generalized Anxiety Disorder Symptom List

Has your child's anxiety or worry been associated with any of the following behaviors for more days than not over the past 6 months? *[Enter 1 if present, 0 if absent, and ? if unknown.]*

[Interviewer: Only one condition needs to be present for this criterion to be met.]

1. Restlessness or feeling keyed up or on edge ____
2. Being easily fatigued or tired ____
3. Difficulty concentrating or mind going blank ____
4. Irritability ____
5. Muscle tension ____
6. Sleep disturbance or difficulties falling asleep, staying asleep, or restless and unsatisfying sleep ____

D. Have these worries created distress for your child or impairment in any of the following areas? *[Enter 1 if present, 0 if absent, and ? if unknown.]*

Social relations with others ____ Academic performance ____

Any other areas of functioning ____

E. Exclusion Criteria: *[Interviewer: Enter 1 if the anxiety or worry are confined to features of another mental disorder, such as being worried about having a panic attack (Panic Disorder), being embarrassed in public (Social Phobia), being contaminated (Obsessive–Compulsive Disorder), being away from home or major attachment figures (Separation Anxiety Disorder), having multiple physical complaints (Somatization Disorder), or having a serious illness (Hypochondriasis); or if the anxiety is associated with Posttraumatic Stress Disorder. Also, enter 1 if the disturbance is due to the direct physiological effects of a substance (e.g., drug abuse, medication) or a general medical condition (e.g., hyperthyroidism) or occurs exclusively during a Mood Disorder, a Psychotic Disorder, or a Pervasive Developmental Disorder. Enter 0 if not, ? if unknown.]* ____

Diagnostic Code

Requirements for diagnosis:

Does section A total 2? ____
Does section B total 1? ____
Does section C total 1 or more? ____
Does section D total 1 or more? ____
Does section E total 0? ____

[Check here if all requirements are met.]

☐ Generalized Anxiety Disorder (300.02)

(cont.)

Dysthymic Disorder

[*Interviewer: Diagnosis requires that depressed mood exist for most of the day, for more days than not, for at least 1 year; that at least two symptoms from B exist; that the child has never been without the symptoms in A and B below for 2 consecutive months during the 1 year of the disturbance; that all exclusionary criteria are met; and that the symptoms cause clinically significant distress or impairment in social, academic, or other important areas of functioning.*]

I would like to speak with you now about your child's mood for most of the time.

A. [*Enter 1 if present, 0 if absent, and ? if unknown.*] Does your child show depressed mood or irritability for most of the day, by either his/her own report or your own observations of your child? ____

Has this depressed mood occurred more days than not for at least the past 12 months? ____

[*Interviewer: If the two questions in A above were endorsed, proceed with remaining criteria for this disorder; otherwise, skip to next disorder. If any of the remaining criteria are not met, skip to the next disorder.*]

B. Does your child show any of the following difficulties while he/she is depressed: [*Enter 1 if present, 0 if absent, and ? if unknown.*]

1. Poor appetite or overeating ____
2. Insomnia (trouble falling asleep) or hypersomnia (excessive sleeping) ____
3. Low energy or fatigue ____
4. Low self-esteem ____
5. Poor concentration or difficulty making decisions ____
6. Feelings of hopelessness ____

C. During the 12 months or more that your child has shown this depressed mood, has he/she ever been without this depressed mood or the other difficulties you mentioned for at least 2 consecutive months? [*Enter 0 if the child has had a 2-month remission, 1 if he/she has not had any remission of symptoms for at least 2 months, and ? if unknown.*] ____

D. Has this depressed mood created distress for your child or impairment in any of the following areas? [*Enter 1 if present, 0 if absent, and ? if unknown.*]

Social relations with others ____ Academic performance ____

Any other areas of functioning ____

E. Exclusion Criteria: [*Interviewer: Enter 1 if the child meets criteria for Major Depressive Episode during the year or more of his/her mood disorder or if the disorder is better accounted for by Major Depressive Disorder. Also, enter 1 if there has ever been a manic episode, mixed manic–depressive episode, or hypomanic episode; or if criteria for Cyclothymic Disorder apply. Enter 1 if the disorder described above occurs exclusively during the course of a chronic Psychotic Disorder Schizophrenia or Delusional Disorder or is the result of the direct physiological effects of a substance or a general medical condition. Enter 0 if not, ? if unknown.*] ____

(cont.)

50

Diagnostic Code

Requirements for diagnosis:

Does section A total 2? ——
Does section B total 2 or more? ——
Does section C total 1? ——
Does section D total 1 or more? ——
Does section E total 0? ——

[Check here if all requirements are met.]

☐ Dysthymic Disorder (300.4)

Major Depressive Disorder

[Interviewer: Diagnosis requires that at least five or more of the symptoms listed in A below have been present for a 2-week period; that this represents a change from previous functioning; that at least one of the symptoms is depressed mood or loss of interest or pleasure; that the symptoms create clinically significant distress or impairment in social, academic, or other important areas of functioning; and that all exclusion criteria are met.]

A. Major Depressive Disorder Symptom List

Let's continue to talk about your child's mood or emotional adjustment. Has your child developed any of the following for at least a 2-week period of time? *[Enter 1 if present, 0 if absent, and ? if unknown.]*

1. Depressed or irritable mood most of the day nearly every day for at least 2 weeks ——
   (This can be by the child's own report or by the parents' or others' observations.)

2. Markedly diminished interest or pleasure in all or almost all activities most of the day, nearly every day for at least 2 weeks ——
   (This can be by the child's own report or by the parents' or others' observations.)
   [Interviewer: If either 1 or 2 was endorsed, proceed with remaining criteria; otherwise, skip to the next disorder.]

3. Significant weight loss, when not dieting ——
   Significant weight gain ——
   Decrease or increase in appetite nearly every day ——
   Failed to meet expected weight gains ——

4. Insomnia (trouble falling asleep) or hypersomnia (excessive sleep) nearly every day ——

5. Agitated or excessive movement nearly every day ——
   (Must be supported by the parents' or others' observations)
   Lethargic, sluggish, slow moving, or significantly reduced movement or activity nearly every day ——
   (Must be supported by the parents' or others' observations)

(cont.)

6. Fatigue or loss of energy nearly every day   ____

7. Feelings of worthlessness or excessive or inappropriate guilt nearly every day   ____
   [*Interviewer: This should not be just self-reproach or guilt about being sick.*]

8. Diminished ability to think or concentrate, or indecisiveness, nearly every day   ____
   (Can be by child's self-report or parent's or others' observations.)

9. Recurrent thoughts of death   ____
   Recurrent thoughts of suicide without a specific plan   ____
   Suicide attempt or a specific plan for committing suicide   ____

[*Interviewer: If five or more of symptoms 1–9 were endorsed, proceed. If not, skip to the next disorder.*]

B. Have these symptoms of depression created distress for your child or impairment in any of the following areas? [*Enter 1 if present, 0 if absent, and ? if unknown.*]

Social relations with others ____ Academic performance ____

Any other areas of functioning ____

C. Exclusion Criteria: [*Interviewer: Enter 1 if the child meets criteria for Bipolar Disorder; if the symptoms are due to direct physiological effects of a substance or a general medical condition; if the symptoms are better accounted for by clinical Bereavement after the loss of a loved one or by Schizoaffective Disorder; if the symptoms are superimposed on Schizophrenia, Schizophreniform Disorder, Delusional Disorder, or Psychotic Disorder NOS; or if there has been a Manic Episode, a Mixed Episode, or a Hypomanic Episode. Enter 0 if not, ? if unknown.*]   ____

Diagnostic Code

Requirements for diagnosis:

Do questions 1 and 2 in section A total 1 or more?   ____
Does section A total 5 or more?   ____
Does section B total 1 or more?   ____
Does section C total 0?   ____

[*Check here if all requirements are met.*]

☐ Major Depressive Disorder (296.xx)
[*Code for single episode is 296.2x, recurrent episodes is 296.3x; see pp. 344–345 of DSM-IV for additional specifications about the disorder.*]

Depressive Disorder, NOS

[*Interviewer: Code this only when there is clinically significant depression with impairment, but when full criteria for Major Depressive Disorder, Dysthymic Disorder, Adjustment Disorder with Depressed Mood, or Adjustment Disorder with Mixed Anxiety and Depressed Mood are not met.*]

☐ Depressive Disorder, NOS (311)

(*cont.*)

Bipolar I Disorder: Manic Episode

[*Interviewer: Diagnosis requires that the child has had a distinct period of at least 1 week of abnormally and persistently elevated, expansive, or irritable mood, or any period of such mood that resulted in hospitalization; and has had at least three of the symptoms listed in B below (or four if mood was primarily irritable) to a significant degree. Also, the symptoms must create clinically significant impairment in social, academic, or other important areas of functioning, and exclusion criteria must be met.*]

I have some more questions to ask you about your child's moods or emotional adjustment.

A. Has your child ever experienced a period of time that lasted at least 1 week: [*Enter 1 if present, 0 if absent, and ? if unknown.*]

1. Where his/her mood was unusually and persistently elevated; that is, he/she felt abnormally happy, giddy, joyous, or ecstatic well beyond normal feelings of happiness? ____

2. Or where his/her mood was abnormally and persistently expansive; that is, your child felt able to accomplish everything he/she decided to do, felt nearly super-human in his/her ability to do anything he/she wished to do, or felt as if his/her abilities were without limits? ____

3. Or where his/her mood was abnormally and persistently irritable; that is, he/she was unusually touchy, too easily prone to anger or temper outbursts, too easily annoyed by events or by others, or abnormally cranky? ____

[*Interviewer: If any of the above three were endorsed, proceed with B; otherwise, skip to next disorder.*]

B. During the week or more that your child showed this abnormal and persistent mood, did you notice any of the following to be persistent and/or occurring to an abnormal or significant degree? [*Enter 1 if present, 0 if absent, and ? if unknown.*]

1. Had inflated self-esteem or felt grandiose about self well beyond what would be characteristic for his/her level of abilities ____

2. Showed a decreased need for sleep; for instance, he/she stated that he/she felt rested after only 3 hours of sleep ____

3. Was more talkative than usual or seemed to feel pressured to keep talking ____

4. Skipped from one idea to another and then another in speech as if his/her ideas were flying rapidly by ____

    Stated that he/she felt that his/her thoughts were racing or flying by at an abnormal rate of speed ____

5. Was distractible; that is, his/her attention was too easily drawn to unimportant or irrelevant events or things around him/her ____

6. Showed an increase in goal-directed activity; that is, he/she became unusually and persistently productive or directed more activity than normal toward the tasks he/she wanted to accomplish ____

    Seemed very agitated, overly active, or abnormally restless ____

(cont.)

53

7. Showed an excessive involvement in pleasurable activities that have a
   high likelihood of negative, harmful, or painful consequences _____

   [*Interviewer: If three or more symptoms above were endorsed, proceed with remaining criteria; otherwise, skip to next disorder.*]

C. [*Enter 1 if present, 0 if absent, and ? if unknown.*]

   1. Was this disturbance in your child's mood enough to cause severe impairment,
      disruption, or difficulties with social relationships, academic performance,
      or other important activities _____

   2. Or, did your child's abnormal mood lead to him/her being hospitalized to
      prevent harm to him/herself or others _____

   3. Or, did your child have hallucinations (explain) or bizarre ideas
      (psychotic thinking), or feel or act paranoid (as if others were intentionally
      out to harm him/her) _____

   [*Interviewer: If one or more of the criteria 1–3 is endorsed, proceed.*]

D. Exclusion Criteria: [*Interviewer: Enter 1 if the symptoms meet criteria for Mixed Manic–Depressive Episode or Schizoaffective Disorder, are the direct physiological effects of a substance or a general medical condition, or are superimposed on Schizophrenia, Schizophreniform Delusional Disorder, or Psychotic Disorder NOS. Enter 0 if not, ? if unknown. Also, if the child meets criteria for ADHD, enter 0 only if the child meets the criteria after excluding distractibility (5, above) and psychomotor agitation (second part of 6, above).*] _____

Diagnostic Code

Requirements for diagnosis:

Does section A total 1 or more? _____
Does section B total 3 or more? _____
Does section C total 1 or more? _____
Does section D total 0? _____

[*Check here if all requirements are met.*]

☐ Bipolar I Disorder: Manic Episode (296.xx)
   [*Code 296.0x if single episode; 296.40 if multiple episodes and most recent was Manic Episode; 296.4x if multiple episodes and most recent was Hypomanic Episode.*]

Bipolar I Disorder: Mixed Episode

[*Interviewer: Code this disorder if criteria are met both for a Manic Episode and for a Major Depressive Episode nearly every day for at least 1 week; disturbance causes clinically significant impairment; and symptoms are not the result of a substance or a general medical condition.*]

☐ Bipolar I Disorder: Mixed Episode (_____)
   [*Code 296.6x if most recent episode is mixed; 296.5x if most recent episode is depressed; 296.7 if most recent episode is unspecified.*]

(*cont.*)

Other Mental and Developmental Disorders

[Enter 1 if present, 0 if absent, and ? if unknown.]

1. Does this child have any things about which he/she seems obsessed or can he/she not get his/her mind off of a particular topic? ____ [If present, review diagnostic criteria for Obsessive–Compulsive Disorder in the DSM-IV.]

2. Does this child have any unusual behaviors he/she must perform, such as dressing, bathing, mealtime, or counting rituals? ____ [If present, review diagnostic criteria for Obsessive–Compulsive disorder in the DSM-IV.]

3. Does this child demonstrate any nervous tics or other repetitive, abrupt nervous movements or vocal noises? ____ [If present, review diagnostic criteria for Tic Disorders or Tourette's Disorder in the DSM-IV.]

4. Has this child made comments or acted in such a way that he/she seemed to see things, hear things, or feel things on his/her skin that really did not exist (hallucinations)? ____ [If present, review diagnostic criteria for Psychotic Disorders in the DSM-IV.]

5. Has this child ever reported bizarre or very strange or peculiar ideas that seemed very unusual compared to other children (delusions)? ____ [If present, review diagnostic criteria for Psychotic Disorders in the DSM-IV.]

PARENT MANAGEMENT METHODS

Now let's move on and talk about how you have tried to manage your child's behavior, especially when it was a problem for you. When your child is disruptive or misbehaves, what steps are you likely to take to deal with the problem?

_____

_____

_____

_____

_____

_____

_____

If these methods do not work and the problem behavior continues, what are you likely to do then to cope with your child's misbehavior?

_____

_____

_____

_____

_____

_____

_____

_____

(cont.)

CHILD'S EVALUATION AND TREATMENT HISTORY

Has your child ever been evaluated previously for developmental, behavioral, or learning problems? [*Circle one*]   Yes   No

If so, who provided the evaluation, what type of evaluation did the child have, and what were you told about your child regarding the results of any evaluations?

_____

_____

_____

_____

_____

Has your child ever received any psychiatric or psychological treatment? [*Circle one*]   Yes   No

If so, what type of treatment did he/she receive and how long did the treatment last?

_____

_____

Who provided this treatment to your child?_____

Has your child ever received any *medication* for his/her behavior or emotional problems? [*Circle one*]   Yes   No

If so, what type of medication did he/she take, at what dose, and for how long?

_____

_____

SCHOOL HISTORY

[*Interviewer: For each grade the child has been in, beginning with preschool, ask the parents which school the child attended and whether the child had any behavioral or learning problems that year, and if so, briefly note their nature below.*]

_____

_____

_____

_____

_____

_____

_____

_____

_____

_____

(cont.)

Has this child ever received any *special education services*? [*Circle one*]   Yes   No

If so, what types of services did he/she receive and in what grades?

_____

_____

_____

_____

CHILD'S PSYCHOLOGICAL AND SOCIAL STRENGTHS

I realize I have asked you a lot about any problems your child might be having. But it is also important that I know about your child's psychological and social strong points. Please tell me about any abilities your child seems to have or any activities at which he/she is particularly good. For instance, what hobbies and sports does your child enjoy and do well at, what are his/her best subjects in school, what sorts of games or social activities does he/she do well in? In other words, tell me what you consider to be your child's strongest or best points.

_____

_____

_____

_____

FAMILY HISTORY

[*Interviewer: After reviewing the child's psychological and social strengths, review with the parent the family history of psychiatric and learning problems, using the following three forms. One form is for the maternal side of the family, the second for the paternal side, and the third for the siblings of the child being evaluated Inform the parent(s) you are interviewing that it is important in under-standing a child's behavioral problems to know whether other biological relatives of the child have had psychological, emotional, or developmental problems. Many such disorders run in families and may contribute genetically to the child's problems. Start with the maternal side of the family and review each of the mother's relatives, noting whether they have any of the disorders listed on the left side of the form. If so, place an X under the column representing that relative. Then do the same for the paternal relatives and the child's siblings.*]

Maternal Relatives

	Self	Mother	Father	Siblings				Total
				Bro	Bro	Sis	Sis	
Problems with aggressiveness, defiance, and oppositional behavior as a child								
Problems with attention, activity, and impulse control as a child								

(*cont.*)

	Self	Mother	Father	Siblings Bro	Bro	Sis	Sis	Total
Learning disabilities								
Failed to graduate from high school								
Mental retardation								
Psychosis or schizophrenia								
Depression for more than 2 weeks								
Anxiety disorder that impaired adjustment								
Tics or Tourette's								
Alcohol abuse								
Substance abuse								
Antisocial behavior (assaults, thefts, etc.)								
Arrests								
Physical abuse								
Sexual abuse								

Paternal Relatives

	Self	Mother	Father	Siblings Bro	Bro	Sis	Sis	Total
Problems with aggressiveness, defiance, and oppositional behavior as a child								
Problems with attention, activity, and impulse control as a child								
Learning disabilities								
Failed to graduate from high school								
Mental retardation								
Psychosis or schizophrenia								
Depression for more than 2 weeks								
Anxiety disorder that impaired adjustment								
Tics or Tourette's								
Alcohol abuse								
Substance abuse								

(cont.)

	Self	Mother	Father	Siblings				Total
				Bro	Bro	Sis	Sis	
Antisocial behavior (assaults, thefts, etc.)								
Arrests								
Physical abuse								
Sexual abuse								

Siblings

	Brother	Brother	Sister	Sister	Total
Problems with aggressiveness, defiance, and oppositional behavior as a child					
Problems with attention, activity, and impulse control as a child					
Learning disabilities					
Failed to graduate from high school					
Mental retardation					
Psychosis or schizophrenia					
Depression for more than 2 weeks					
Anxiety disorder that impaired adjustment					
Tics or Tourette's					
Alcohol abuse					
Substance abuse					
Antisocial behavior (assaults, thefts, etc.)					
Arrests					
Physical abuse					
Sexual abuse					

DISRUPTIVE BEHAVIOR RATING SCALE—PARENT FORM

Child's name_____ **Date**_____

Name of person completing this form_____

Your relationship to child: [*Circle one*]   Mother   Father   Stepparent   Fosterparent
Other:_____

Instructions: Please circle the number next to each item that best describes the behavior of this child *during the past 6 months*.

Items:	Never or rarely	Sometimes	Often	Very often
1. Fails to give close attention to details or makes careless mistakes in his/her work	0	1	2	3
2. Fidgets with hands or feet or squirms in seat	0	1	2	3
3. Has difficulty sustaining his/her attention in tasks or fun activities	0	1	2	3
4. Leaves his/her seat in classroom or in other situations in which seating is expected	0	1	2	3
5. Doesn't listen when spoken to directly	0	1	2	3
6. Seems restless	0	1	2	3
7. Doesn't follow through on instructions and fails to finish work	0	1	2	3
8. Has difficulty engaging in leisure activities or doing fun things quietly	0	1	2	3
9. Has difficulty organizing tasks and activities	0	1	2	3
10. Seems "on the go" or "driven by a motor"	0	1	2	3
11. Avoids, dislikes, or is reluctant to engage in work that requires sustained mental effort	0	1	2	3
12. Talks excessively	0	1	2	3
13. Loses things necessary for tasks or activities	0	1	2	3
14. Blurts out answers before questions have been completed	0	1	2	3

(*cont.*)

From *Attention-Deficit Hyperactivity Disorder: A Clinical Workbook* (2nd ed.) by Russell A. Barkley and Kevin R. Murphy. Copyright 1998 by The Guilford Press. Permission to photocopy this form is granted to purchasers of the *Workbook* for personal use only (see copyright page for details).

Items:	Never or rarely	Sometimes	Often	Very often
15. Is easily distracted	0	1	2	3
16. Has difficulty awaiting turn	0	1	2	3
17. Is forgetful in daily activities	0	1	2	3
18. Interrupts or intrudes on others	0	1	2	3

How old was this child when you first noticed the above problems? _____

Instructions: To what extent do the problems you may have circled on the previous page interfere with this child's ability to function in each of these areas of life activities *during the past 6 months?*

Areas:	Never or rarely	Sometimes	Often	Very often
In his/her home life with the immediate family	0	1	2	3
In his/her social interactions with other children	0	1	2	3
In his/her activities or dealings in the community	0	1	2	3
In school	0	1	2	3
In sports, clubs, or other organizations	0	1	2	3
In learning to take care of him/herself	0	1	2	3
In his/her play, leisure, or recreational activities	0	1	2	3
In his/her handling of daily chores or other responsibilities	0	1	2	3

Instructions: Again, please circle the number next to each item that best describes the behavior of this child *during the past 6 months.*

Items:	Never or rarely	Sometimes	Often	Very often
19. Loses temper	0	1	2	3
20. Argues with adults	0	1	2	3
21. Actively defies or refuses to comply with adults' requests or rules	0	1	2	3
22. Deliberately annoys people	0	1	2	3
23. Blames others for his/her mistakes or misbehavior	0	1	2	3
24. Is touchy or easily annoyed by others	0	1	2	3

(cont.)

Items:	Never or rarely	Sometimes	Often	Very often
25. Is angry or resentful	0	1	2	3
26. Is spiteful or vindictive	0	1	2	3

Instructions: Please indicate whether this child has engaged in any of the following items in the past 12 months.

1. Often bullies, threatens, or intimidates others	No	Yes
2. Often initiates physical fights	No	Yes
3. Used a weapon that can cause serious physical harm to others (e.g., a bat, brick, broken bottle, knife, or gun)	No	Yes
4. Has been physically cruel to people	No	Yes
5. Has been physically cruel to animals	No	Yes
6. Has stolen while confronting a victim (e.g., mugging, purse snatching, extortion, or armed robbery)	No	Yes
7. Has forced someone into sexual activity	No	Yes
8. Has deliberately engaged in fire setting with the intention of causing serious damage	No	Yes
9. Has deliberately destroyed others' property (other than by fire setting)	No	Yes
10. Has broken into someone else's house, building, or car	No	Yes
11. Often lies to obtain goods or favors or to avoid obligations (i.e., "cons" others)	No	Yes
12. Has stolen items of nontrivial value without confronting a victim (e.g., shoplifting, but without breaking and entering, and forgery)	No	Yes
13. Often stays out at night despite parental prohibitions If so, at what age did this begin?_____	No	Yes
14. Has run away from home overnight at least twice while living in parents' home, foster care, or group home. If so, how many times?_____	No	Yes
15. Is often truant from school If so, at what age did this begin_____	No	Yes

DISRUPTIVE BEHAVIOR RATING SCALE—TEACHER FORM

Child's name_____ Date_____

Name of person completing this form_____

What class(es) do you teach this child?_____

In a typical school day, how many hours do you observe this child?_____

Instructions: Please circle the number next to each item that best describes the behavior of this child *during the past 6 months.*

Items:	Never or rarely	Sometimes	Often	Very often
1. Fails to give close attention to details or makes careless mistakes in his/her work	0	1	2	3
2. Fidgets with hands or feet or squirms in seat	0	1	2	3
3. Has difficulty sustaining his/her attention in tasks or fun activities	0	1	2	3
4. Leaves his/her seat in classroom or in other situations in which seating is expected	0	1	2	3
5. Doesn't listen when spoken to directly	0	1	2	3
6. Seems restless	0	1	2	3
7. Doesn't follow through on instructions and fails to finish work	0	1	2	3
8. Has difficulty engaging in leisure activities or doing fun things quietly	0	1	2	3
9. Has difficulty organizing tasks and activities	0	1	2	3
10. Seems "on the go" or "driven by a motor"	0	1	2	3
11. Avoids, dislikes, or is reluctant to engage in work that requires sustained mental effort	0	1	2	3
12. Talks excessively	0	1	2	3
13. Loses things necessary for tasks or activities	0	1	2	3
14. Blurts out answers before questions have been completed	0	1	2	3
15. Is easily distracted	0	1	2	3

(cont.)

From *Attention-Deficit Hyperactivity Disorder: A Clinical Workbook* (2nd ed.) by Russell A. Barkley and Kevin R. Murphy. Copyright 1998 by The Guilford Press. Permission to photocopy this form is granted to purchasers of the *Workbook* for personal use only (see copyright page for details).

Items:	Never or rarely	Sometimes	Often	Very often
16. Has difficulty awaiting turn	0	1	2	3
17. Is forgetful in daily activities	0	1	2	3
18. Interrupts or intrudes on others	0	1	2	3

Instructions: To what extent do the problems you may have circled on the previous page interfere with this child's ability to function in each of these areas of school activities *during the past 6 months?*

Areas:	Never or rarely	Sometimes	Often	Very often
In his/her completion of classwork	0	1	2	3
In his/her completion of homework assignments	0	1	2	3
In his/her behavior in the school classroom	0	1	2	3
In his/her behavior on the school bus	0	1	2	3
In sports, clubs, or other organizations held at school	0	1	2	3
In his/her interactions with classmates	0	1	2	3
In his/her play or recreational activities at recess	0	1	2	3
In his/her behavior in the lunchroom at school	0	1	2	3
In his/her management of time at school	0	1	2	3

Instructions: Again, please circle the number next to each item that best describes the behavior of this child *during the past 6 months.*

Items:	Never or rarely	Sometimes	Often	Very often
19. Loses temper	0	1	2	3
20. Argues with adults	0	1	2	3
21. Actively defies or refuses to comply with adults' requests or rules	0	1	2	3
22. Deliberately annoys people	0	1	2	3
23. Blames others for his/her mistakes or misbehavior	0	1	2	3
24. Is touchy or easily annoyed by others	0	1	2	3
25. Is angry or resentful	0	1	2	3
26. Is spiteful or vindictive	0	1	2	3

HOME SITUATIONS QUESTIONNAIRE

Child's name_____ Date_____

Name of person completing this form_____

Instructions: Does your child present any problems with compliance to instructions, commands, or rules for you in any of these situations? If so, please circle the word Yes and then circle a number beside that situation that describes how severe the problem is for you. If your child is not a problem in a situation, circle No and go on to the next situation on the form.

Situations	Yes/No		If yes, how severe?								
			Mild								Severe
While playing alone	Yes	No	1	2	3	4	5	6	7	8	9
While playing with other children	Yes	No	1	2	3	4	5	6	7	8	9
At mealtimes	Yes	No	1	2	3	4	5	6	7	8	9
Getting dressed	Yes	No	1	2	3	4	5	6	7	8	9
Washing and bathing	Yes	No	1	2	3	4	5	6	7	8	9
While you are on the telephone	Yes	No	1	2	3	4	5	6	7	8	9
While watching television	Yes	No	1	2	3	4	5	6	7	8	9
When visitors are in your home	Yes	No	1	2	3	4	5	6	7	8	9
When you are visiting someone's home	Yes	No	1	2	3	4	5	6	7	8	9
In public places (restaurants, stores, church, etc.)	Yes	No	1	2	3	4	5	6	7	8	9
When father is home	Yes	No	1	2	3	4	5	6	7	8	9
When asked to do chores	Yes	No	1	2	3	4	5	6	7	8	9
When asked to do homework	Yes	No	1	2	3	4	5	6	7	8	9
At bedtime	Yes	No	1	2	3	4	5	6	7	8	9
While in the car	Yes	No	1	2	3	4	5	6	7	8	9
When with a babysitter	Yes	No	1	2	3	4	5	6	7	8	9

- For Office Use Only -

Total number of problem settings_____ Mean severity score_____

From *Defiant Children* (2nd ed.): *A Clinician's Manual for Assessment and Parent Training* by Russell A. Barkley. Copyright 1997 by The Guilford Press. Reprinted in *Attention-Deficit Hyperactivity Disorder: A Clinical Workbook* (2nd ed.) by Russell A. Barkley and Kevin R. Murphy. Permission to photocopy this form is granted to purchasers of the *Workbook* for personal use only (see copyright page for details).

SCHOOL SITUATIONS QUESTIONNAIRE

Child's name_____ Date_____

Name of person completing this form_____

Instructions: Does this child present any problems with compliance to instructions, commands, or rules for you in any of these situations? If so, please circle the word Yes and then circle a number beside that situation that describes how severe the problem is for you. If this child is not a problem in a situation, circle No and go on to the next situation on the form.

Situations	Yes/No		Mild								Severe
When arriving at school	Yes	No	1	2	3	4	5	6	7	8	9
During individual desk work	Yes	No	1	2	3	4	5	6	7	8	9
During small group activities	Yes	No	1	2	3	4	5	6	7	8	9
During free playtime in class	Yes	No	1	2	3	4	5	6	7	8	9
During lectures to the class	Yes	No	1	2	3	4	5	6	7	8	9
At recess	Yes	No	1	2	3	4	5	6	7	8	9
At lunch	Yes	No	1	2	3	4	5	6	7	8	9
In the hallways	Yes	No	1	2	3	4	5	6	7	8	9
In the bathroom	Yes	No	1	2	3	4	5	6	7	8	9
On field trips	Yes	No	1	2	3	4	5	6	7	8	9
During special assemblies	Yes	No	1	2	3	4	5	6	7	8	9
On the bus	Yes	No	1	2	3	4	5	6	7	8	9

If yes, how severe?

- For Office Use Only -

Total number of problem settings_____ Mean severity score_____

From *Defiant Children* (2nd ed.): *A Clinician's Manual for Assessment and Parent Training* by Russell A. Barkley. Copyright 1997 by The Guilford Press. Reprinted in *Attention-Deficit Hyperactivity Disorder: A Clinical Workbook* (2nd ed.) by Russell A. Barkley and Kevin R. Murphy. Permission to photocopy this form is granted to purchasers of the *Workbook* for personal use only (see copyright page for details).

ISSUES CHECKLIST FOR PARENTS AND TEENAGERS

Name_____ Date_____

☐ Adolescent		☐ Adolescent
☐ Mother	*with*	☐ Mother
☐ Father		☐ Father

Below is a list of things that sometimes get talked about at home. We would like you to look carefully at each topic on the left-hand side of the page and decide whether the *two of you together* have talked about that topic at *all* during the last 2 weeks.

If the two of you together have discussed it during the last 2 weeks, circle *Yes* to the right of the topic.

If the two of you together have *not* discussed it during the last 2 weeks, circle No to the right of the topic.

Now, we would like you to go back over the list of topics. For those topics for which you circled Yes, please answer the two questions on the right-hand side of the page.

1. How many times during the last 2 weeks did the topic come up?
2. How hot are the discussions?

Go down this column for all pages first.   Then go down these columns for all pages.

| Topic | | | How many times? | How hot are the discussions? | | | | |
				Calm	A little angry		Angry	
1. Telephone calls	Yes	No		1	2	3	4	5
2. Time for going to bed	Yes	No		1	2	3	4	5
3. Cleaning up bedroom	Yes	No		1	2	3	4	5
4. Doing homework	Yes	No		1	2	3	4	5
5. Putting away clothes	Yes	No		1	2	3	4	5
6. Using the television	Yes	No		1	2	3	4	5

(cont.)

Adapted from *Negotiating Parent–Adolescent Conflict: A Behavioral–Family Systems Approach* by Arthur L. Robin and Sharon L. Foster. Copyright 1989 by The Guilford Press. Reprinted in *Attention-Deficit Hyperactivity Disorder: A Clinical Workbook* (2nd ed.) by Russell A. Barkley and Kevin R. Murphy. Permission to photocopy this form is granted to purchasers of the *Workbook* for personal use only (see copyright page for details).

Topic			How many times?	Calm		A little angry		Angry
7. Cleanliness (washing, showers, brushing teeth)	Yes	No		1	2	3	4	5
8. Which clothes to wear	Yes	No		1	2	3	4	5
9. How neat clothing looks	Yes	No		1	2	3	4	5
10. Making too much noise at home	Yes	No		1	2	3	4	5
11. Table manners	Yes	No		1	2	3	4	5
12. Fighting with brothers or sisters	Yes	No		1	2	3	4	5
13. Cursing	Yes	No		1	2	3	4	5
14. How money is spent	Yes	No		1	2	3	4	5
15. Picking books or movies	Yes	No		1	2	3	4	5
16. Allowance	Yes	No		1	2	3	4	5
17. Going places without parents (shopping, movies, etc.)	Yes	No		1	2	3	4	5
18. Playing stereo or radio too loudly	Yes	No		1	2	3	4	5
19. Turning off lights in house	Yes	No		1	2	3	4	5
20. Drugs	Yes	No		1	2	3	4	5
21. Taking care of records, games, toys, and things	Yes	No		1	2	3	4	5
22. Drinking beer or other liquor	Yes	No		1	2	3	4	5
23. Buying records, games, toys, and things	Yes	No		1	2	3	4	5
24. Going on dates	Yes	No		1	2	3	4	5
25. Who should be friends	Yes	No		1	2	3	4	5
26. Selecting new clothing	Yes	No		1	2	3	4	5
27. Sex	Yes	No		1	2	3	4	5
28. Coming home on time	Yes	No		1	2	3	4	5
29. Getting to school on time	Yes	No		1	2	3	4	5
30. Getting low grades in school	Yes	No		1	2	3	4	5
31. Getting in trouble in school	Yes	No		1	2	3	4	5

(cont.)

Topic			How many times?	Calm		A little angry		Angry
32. Lying	Yes	No		1	2	3	4	5
33. Helping out around the house	Yes	No		1	2	3	4	5
34. Talking back to parents	Yes	No		1	2	3	4	5
35. Getting up in the morning	Yes	No		1	2	3	4	5
36. Bothering parents when they want to be left alone	Yes	No		1	2	3	4	5
37. Bothering teenager when he/she wants to be left alone	Yes	No		1	2	3	4	5
38. Putting feet on furniture	Yes	No		1	2	3	4	5
39. Messing up the house	Yes	No		1	2	3	4	5
40. What time to have meals	Yes	No		1	2	3	4	5
41. How to spend free time	Yes	No		1	2	3	4	5
42. Smoking	Yes	No		1	2	3	4	5
43. Earning money away from house	Yes	No		1	2	3	4	5
44. What teenager eats	Yes	No		1	2	3	4	5

Check to see that you circled Yes or No for every topic. Then tell the interviewer you are finished.

USING A DAILY SCHOOL BEHAVIOR REPORT CARD

A daily school behavior report card involves having the teacher send home an evaluation of your child's behavior in school that day, which can be used by you to give or take away rewards available at home. These cards have been shown to be effective in modifying a wide range of problems with children at school. Due to their convenience and cost-effectiveness and the fact that they involve both the teacher(s) and parents, they are often one of the first interventions you should try if behavior problems at school are occurring with your child. The teacher reports can consist of either a note or a more formal report card. We recommend the use of a formal behavior report card like those shown at the end of this handout. The card should list the "target" behavior(s) that are to be the focus of the program on the left-hand side of the card. Across the top should be numbered columns that correspond to each class period at school. The teacher gives a number rating reflecting how well the child did for each of these behaviors for each class period. Some examples are provided at the end of this handout.

HOW THE DAILY REPORT CARD WORKS

Using this system, teacher reports are typically sent home on a daily basis. As the child's behavior improves, the daily reports can be reduced to twice weekly (Wednesdays and Fridays), once weekly, or even monthly, and finally phased out altogether. A variety of daily report cards may be developed and tailored for your child. Some of the behaviors targeted for the program may include both social conduct (shares, plays well with peers, follows rules) and academic performance (completes math or reading assignments). Targeting low academic performance (poor production of work) may be especially effective. Examples of behaviors to target include completing all (or a specified portion of) work, staying in the assigned seat, following teacher directions, and playing cooperatively with others. Negative behaviors (e.g., aggression, destruction, calling out) may also be included as target behaviors to be reduced by the program. In addition to targeting class performance, homework may be included. Children sometimes have difficulty remembering to bring homework assignments home. They may also complete their homework but forget to return the completed work to school the next day. Each of these areas may be targeted in a school behavior report card program.

It is recommended that the number of target behaviors you work on be kept to about four or five. Start out by focusing on just a few behaviors you wish to change, to help maximize your child's success in the program. When these behaviors are going well, you can add a few more problem behaviors as targets for change. We recommend including at least one or two positive behaviors that the child is currently doing well with, so that the child will be able to earn some points during the beginning of the program.

(cont.)

From *Defiant Children* (2nd ed.): *A Clinician's Manual for Assessment and Parent Training* by Russell A. Barkley. Copyright 1997 by The Guilford Press. Reprinted in *Attention-Deficit Hyperactivity Disorder: A Clinical Workbook* (2nd ed.) by Russell A. Barkley and Kevin R. Murphy. Permission to photocopy this form is granted to purchasers of the *Workbook* for personal use only (see copyright page for details).

Typically, children are monitored throughout the school day. However, to be successful with problem behaviors that occur very frequently, you may want to have the child initially rated for only a portion of the school day, such as for one or two subjects or classes. As the child's behavior improves, the card can be expanded gradually to include more periods/subjects until the child is being monitored throughout the day. In cases where children attend several different classes taught by different teachers, the program may involve some or all of the teachers, depending on the need for help in each of the classes. When more than one teacher is included in the program, a single report card may include space for all teachers to rate the child. Alternatively, different report cards may be used for each class and organized in a notebook for children to carry between classes. Again, the card shown at the end of this handout can be helpful because it has columns that can be used to rate the child by the same teacher at the end of each subject, or by different teachers.

The success of the program depends on a clear, consistent method for translating the teacher's reports into consequences at home. One advantage of school behavior report cards is that a wide variety of consequences can be used. At a minimum, praise and positive attention should be provided at home whenever a child does well that day at school, as shown on the report card. With many children, however, tangible rewards or token programs are often necessary. For example, a positive note home may translate into television time, a special snack, or a later bedtime. A token system may also be used in which a child earns points for positive behavior ratings and loses points for negative ratings. Both daily rewards (e.g., time with parent, special dessert, television time) and weekly rewards (e.g., movie, dinner at a restaurant, special outing) may be included in the program.

ADVANTAGES OF THE DAILY REPORT CARD

Overall, daily school behavior report cards can be as or even more effective than classroom-based behavior management programs, with effectiveness increased when combined with classroom based programs. Daily reports seem particularly well suited for children because the children often benefit from the more frequent feedback than is usually provided at school. These programs also give parents more frequent feedback than would normally be provided by the child. As you know, most children, when asked how their school day went, give you a one-word answer, "Fine," which may not be accurate. These report card programs also can remind parents when to reward a child's behavior, and forewarn parents when behavior is becoming a problem at school and will require more intensive work. In addition, the type and quality of rewards available in the home are usually far more extensive than those available in the classroom, a factor that may be critical with children who need more powerful rewards.

Aside from these benefits, daily school report cards generally require much less time and effort from your child's teacher than do classroom-based programs. As a result, teachers who have been unable to start a classroom management program may be far more likely to cooperate with a daily report card that comes from home.

Despite the impressive success of report card programs, the effectiveness of the program depends on the teacher accurately evaluating the child's behavior. It also hinges on the fair and consistent

(cont.)

use of consequences at home. In some cases, children may attempt to undercut the system by failing to bring home a report. They may forge a teacher's signature or fail to get a certain teacher's signature. To discourage these practices, missing notes or signatures should be treated the same way as a "bad" report (i.e., child fails to earn points or is fined by losing privileges or points). The child may even be grounded for the day (no privileges) for not bringing the card home.

SOME EXAMPLES OF DAILY SCHOOL REPORT CARDS

Several types of school behavior report cards that rely on daily school behavior ratings will be discussed here. Two examples are provided at the end of this handout, as well as a blank card for you to modify as you see fit. These are the cards we recommend most parents use if they want to start a school behavior report card quickly. One sample card is for classroom behavior, the other is for recess behavior. Use whichever sample card is most appropriate for the problems your child is having at school, or fill in the blank card with the specific problems that you want to have evaluated. Two sets of each card are provided so that you can make photocopies of that page and then cut the page in half to make double the number of cards.

Notice that each card contains five areas of potential behavior problems that children may experience. For the class behavior report card, columns are provided for up to seven different teachers to rate the child in these areas of behavior or for one teacher to rate the child many times across the school day. We have found that the more frequent the ratings, the more effective is the feedback for the children and the more informative the program is to you. The teacher initials the bottom of the column after rating the child's performance during that class period to ensure against forgery. If getting the correct homework assignment home is a problem for some children, the teacher can require the child to copy the homework for that class period on the back of the card before completing the ratings for that period. In this way, the teacher merely checks the back of the card for the child's accuracy in copying the assignment and then completes the ratings on the front of the card. For particularly negative ratings, we also encourage teachers to provide a brief explanation to you as to what resulted in that negative mark. The teachers rate the children using a 5-point system (1 = excellent, 2 = good, 3 = fair, 4 = poor, and 5 = very poor).

The child takes a new card to school each day. These can be kept at school and a new card given out each morning, or you can provide the card as your child leaves for school, whichever is most likely to be done consistently. As soon as the child returns home, you should immediately inspect the card, discuss the positive ratings first with your child, and then proceed to a neutral, business-like (not angry!) discussion with your child about any negative marks and the reason for them. Your child should then be asked to formulate a plan for how to avoid getting a negative mark tomorrow. You are to remind your child of this plan the next morning before your child departs for school. After the child formulates the plan, you should award your child points for each rating on the card and deduct points for each negative mark. For instance, a young elementary school-age child may receive five chips for a 1, three for a 2, and one chip for a 3, while being fined three chips for a 4 and five chips for a 5 on the card. For older children, the points might be 25, 15, 5, –15, and –25, respectively, for marks 1–5 on the card. The chips or points are then added up, the

(cont.)

fines are subtracted, and the child may then spend what is left of these chips on the privileges on the home reward menu.

Another daily report card program is provided for dealing with behavior problems and getting along with others during school recess periods or free time periods each day. Again, two cards are provided on the page so that you can make photocopies of the page and cut the pages in half to double the number of cards. The card is to be completed by the teacher on recess duty during each recess or free time period. It is inspected by the class teacher when the child returns to the classroom, and then should be sent home for use, as above, in a home chip/point system. The classroom teacher should also be instructed to use a "think aloud–think ahead" procedure with the child just prior to the child's going out for recess or free time. In this procedure, the teacher (1) reviews the rules for proper recess behavior with the child and notes that they are written on the card, (2) reminds the child that he/she is being watched by the teacher on recess duty, and (3) directs the child to give the card immediately to the recess monitor so the monitor can evaluate the child's behavior during recess or free time.

As these cards illustrate, virtually any child behavior can be the target for treatment using behavior report cards. If the cards shown here are not suited for your child's behavior problems at school, then design a new card with the assistance of your therapist, using the blank cards provided at the end of this handout. They do not take long to construct and can be very helpful in improving a child's school behavior and performance.

DAILY SCHOOL BEHAVIOR REPORT CARD

Child's name_____ Date_____

Teachers:

Please rate this child's behavior today in the areas listed below. Use a separate column for each subject or class period. Use the following ratings: 1 = excellent, 2 = good, 3 = fair, 4 = poor, and 5 = very poor. Then initial the box at the bottom of your column. Add any comments about the child's behavior today on the back of this card.

	Class periods/subjects						
Behaviors to be rated:	1	2	3	4	5	6	7
Class participation							
Performance of class work							
Follows classroom rules							
Gets along well with other children							
Quality of homework, if any given							
Teacher's initials							

Place comments on back of card

- Cut here after photocopying -

DAILY SCHOOL BEHAVIOR REPORT CARD

Child's name_____ Date_____

Teachers:

Please rate this child's behavior today in the areas listed below. Use a separate column for each subject or class period. Use the following ratings: 1 = excellent, 2 = good, 3 = fair, 4 = poor, and 5 = very poor. Then initial the box at the bottom of your column. Add any comments about the child's behavior today on the back of this card.

	Class periods/subjects						
Behaviors to be rated:	1	2	3	4	5	6	7
Class participation							
Performance of class work							
Follows classroom rules							
Gets along well with other children							
Quality of homework, if any given							
Teacher's initials							

Place comments on back of card

DAILY RECESS AND FREE TIME BEHAVIOR REPORT CARD

Child's name_____ Date_____

Teachers:

Please rate this child's behavior today during recess or other free time periods in the areas listed below. Use a separate column for each recess/free time period. Use the following ratings: 1 = excellent, 2 = good, 3 = fair, 4 = poor, and 5 = very poor. Then initial at the bottom of the column. Add any comments on the back.

Behaviors to be rated:	Recess and free time periods				
	1	2	3	4	5
Keeps hands to self; does not push, shove					
Does not tease others; no taunting/put-downs					
Follows recess/free time rules					
Gets along well with other children					
Does not fight or hit; no kicking or punching					
Teacher's initials					

Place comments on back of card

- Cut here after photocopying -

DAILY RECESS AND FREE TIME BEHAVIOR REPORT CARD

Child's name_____ Date_____

Teachers:

Please rate this child's behavior today during recess or other free time periods in the areas listed below. Use a separate column for each recess/free time period. Use the following ratings: 1 = excellent, 2 = good, 3 = fair, 4 = poor, and 5 = very poor. Then initial at the bottom of the column. Add any comments on the back.

Behaviors to be rated:	Daily recess and free time periods				
	1	2	3	4	5
Keeps hands to self; does not push, shove					
Does not tease others; no taunting/put-downs					
Follows recess or free time rules					
Gets along well with other children					
Does not fight or hit; no kicking or punching					
Teacher's initials					

Place comments on back of card

DAILY SCHOOL BEHAVIOR REPORT CARD

Child's name_____ Date_____

Teachers:

Please rate this child's behavior today in the areas listed below. Use a separate column for each subject or class period. Use the following ratings: 1 = excellent, 2 = good, 3 = fair, 4 = poor, and 5 = very poor. Then initial the box at the bottom of your column. Add any comments about the child's behavior today on the back of this card.

Behaviors to be rated:	Class periods/subjects						
	1	2	3	4	5	6	7
_____							
_____							
_____							
_____							
Teacher's initials							

Place comments on back of card

- Cut here after photocopying -

DAILY SCHOOL BEHAVIOR REPORT CARD

Child's name_____ Date_____

Teachers:

Please rate this child's behavior today in the areas listed below. Use a separate column for each subject or class period. Use the following ratings: 1 = excellent, 2 = good, 3 = fair, 4 = poor, and 5 = very poor. Then initial the box at the bottom of your column. Add any comments about the child's behavior today on the back of this card.

Behaviors to be rated:	Class periods/subjects						
	1	2	3	4	5	6	7
_____							
_____							
_____							
_____							
Teacher's initials							

Place comments on back of card

Forms for the Evaluation of Adults

Instructions for Adult Forms

The forms contained in this section are designed to be used in the assessment of adults seeking evaluation of Attention-Deficit/Hyperactivity Disorder (ADHD). Before utilizing these instruments in your professional practice, we recommend that you become familiar with the chapter on assessment of adults by Kevin R. Murphy, PhD, and Michael Gordon, PhD, in the text by Barkley, *Attention-Deficit Hyperactivity Disorder: A Handbook for Diagnosis and Treatment* (2nd ed., Guilford Press, 1998).

Following requests for an evaluation, you may wish to send out the following forms to be completed by adult clients concerned about ADHD prior to their scheduled appointment. Indeed, we recommend that you stipulate that these scales be completed and returned to you before you provide the patient with his/her scheduled appointment, provided, of course, you are working in an outpatient setting: the Developmental Employment, Health, and Social History forms; the Current Symptoms Scale—Self-Report Form; the Childhood Symptoms Scale—Self-Report Form; and the Work Performance Rating Scale—Self-Report Form. The Current Symptoms and Childhood Symptoms forms assess the symptoms of ADHD, currently and retrospectively in childhood, from the client's perspective. Norms and scoring instructions for these self-reports of ADHD symptoms are provided below.

At the time that clients contact you for an evaluation, we recommend that you immediately obtain their permission to send the Current Symptoms Scale—Other Report Form to someone who knows them well currently, such as a spouse, live-in partner, parent, sibling, or close friend whom the client trusts to give a fair reporting of their current status. In addition, we strongly recommend that you send both the Childhood Symptoms Scale—Other Report Form and the Childhood School Performance Scale—Other Report Form to someone who knew the client well as a child. Preferably, this will be a parent, if available. Otherwise, a sibling or close friend since childhood may suffice. Although norms are not available for these forms when completed by others, the forms may still yield a clinically rich vein of information about the client and provide the corroborative information essential in the evaluation of adults for ADHD.

Also contained in this part of the workbook is an interview form you may wish to employ in your clinical interview with the client. It contains most of the information we seek from our own clients at the Adult ADHD Clinic at the University of Massachusetts Medical Center. Although it does not cover all the DSM-IV Axis I disorders an adult may experience, it covers those disorders we have found to occur most frequently in adults with ADHD seen at our own clinic.

Scoring the Current Symptoms Scale—Self Report Form

This scale contains the 18 symptom items for ADHD from DSM-IV cast in the form of a self-report rating scale. These comprise the first page of the scale. On later pages, the scale also contains questions pertaining to age of onset of symptoms and areas in which the client believes the symptoms are leading to impairment in major life activities. At the end of the scale are the 8 items for Oppositional Defiant Disorder (ODD) from DSM-IV. We find that many adults who may have had this disorder as a child, along with their ADHD, are likely to retain some of their hostile–defiant behavioral pattern into adulthood. Thus we believe it is important to collect information on these symptoms as some of the impairment the individual may be experiencing in interpersonal relations and employment may stem from these symptoms continuing to be present in adulthood.

We have collected some local norms for adults residing in central Massachusetts based on a sample of convenience of 720 adults renewing their driver's licenses. At the time we collected these norms, all adult drivers in this state were required to renew their licenses in person, making this method of data collection a convenient means of acquiring a relatively representative sample of adults in this area. For more information on this study, see Murphy and Barkley (1996). The reader is hereby cautioned that these norms may not be representative of other geographic regions. Nevertheless, given that norms for other regions are not yet available, the data provided here can at least be used to provide a very rough indication of how deviant your client may be on these scales, at least in comparison to our geographic region.

Three approaches can be used to score this scale. We recommend you examine all three as each approach has its own limitations.

Symptom Count Compared to DSM-IV Criteria

The 18 symptoms for ADHD are arranged in this scale such that the items pertaining to inattention are the odd-numbered items (1, 3, 5, 7, . . .) and those pertaining to hyperactive–impulsive symptoms are even-numbered items (2, 4, 6, 8, . . .). These two lists of symptoms should be scored separately no matter which of these approaches you are using to score this rating scale. Simply count the number of items that have been answered 2 (Often) or 3 (Very often) for the inattention items (odd-numbered). If it is six or more, this score can be considered clinically significant as it exceeds the recommended threshold of six out of nine symptoms for this list given in DSM-IV. Now do the same for the hyperactive–impulsive items (even numbered). Again, if the score is six or more, this meets the DSM-IV threshold of six of nine symptoms for this symptom list. Individuals who only meet the threshold for one of these lists may possibly have that subtype of ADHD (Predominantly Inattentive or Predominantly Hyperactive–Impulsive). Those meeting criteria for both lists may possibly have the Combined subtype. Of course, a score on a rating scale alone is not sufficient to render a clinical diagnosis of ADHD, but such scores may be consistent with the presence of this disorder indicating that further clinical evaluation for the disorder is indicated. At the very least, these scores indicate which cluster of symptoms of ADHD are most problematic for this client (inattention and/or hyperactive–impulsive behavior).

For the eight symptoms representing ODD provided at the end of this rating scale, you may follow this same approach. Count the number of items answered with a 2 or 3. If it is 4 or higher, this exceeds the DSM-IV threshold for this disorder.

This scoring approach indicates whether the client meets or exceeds DSM-IV recommended thresholds for each of these symptom lists. Some caution is in order, however, in interpreting scores that do not meet or exceed this six-of-nine threshold for ADHD or the four-of-eight threshold for ODD. Such scores do not necessarily reflect normal functioning, nor do they rule out the presence of either of these disorders. This is because the DSM-IV thresholds were developed on children (ages 4–16 years) and may not be as sensitive to either disorder as it is expressed in adults. Our research suggests that the DSM-IV thresholds may be overly restrictive or excessively deviant for adults, representing a threshold that is far more deviant relative to adults than it is relative to children. And so we recommend that you undertake the following two scoring approaches as well.

Symptom Count Relative to Adult Norms

In this approach, score the rating scale precisely the same way as above. Then consult the accompanying table of norms to see whether the number of symptoms for each list (inattention, hyperactive–impulsive, ODD) meets or exceeds the threshold of 1.5 standard deviations ($+1.5\ SD$) above the mean for the client's age group. This score can be found in that column of the table headed $+1.5\ SD$). This threshold represents approximately the 93rd percentile and is often used as an indication of whether a score on a rating scale is clinically significant. Both males and females are included together in this table of norms as we found no significant differences as a function of gender in our study of this sample of adults. Given the small sample sizes for adults over 50 years of age in these tables, use great caution in interpreting these thresholds as indications of deviance.

This scoring approach tells you whether the client is experiencing more symptoms than the general adult population (at least that in our region). Unfortunately, this approach loses some valuable information because it ignores any symptoms answered as a 1 (Sometimes). Yet researchers have come to recognize that each of the two symptom lists for

Means, Standard Deviations, and Deviance Thresholds (+1.5 *SD*) by Age Group for the Positive Symptom Counts for the ADHD and ODD Current Symptoms Collapsed across Gender

Symptom	Age (in years)	Mean	SD	+1.5 SD cutoff	N
Inattention	17–29	1.3	1.8	4.0	275
Inattention	30–49	0.9	1.6	3.3	316
Inattention	50+	0.4	1.0	1.9	90
Hyper.–Impulsive	17–29	2.1	2.0	5.1	276
Hyper.–Impulsive	30–49	1.5	1.8	4.2	309
Hyper.–Impulsive	50+	0.8	1.3	2.8	93
Total ADHD score	17–29	3.3	3.5	8.6	266
Total ADHD score	30–49	2.3	2.9	6.7	299
Total ADHD score	50+	1.2	2.0	4.2	87
ODD score	17–29	1.2	1.8	3.9	271
ODD score	30–49	0.6	1.4	2.7	308
ODD score	50+	0.2	0.9	1.6	91

Note. *N*, sample size; *SD*, standard deviation.

ADHD, and even that for ODD, probably, represents dimensions of behavior. To better capture this dimensional nature of behavior, all the answers to the items on the scale should be utilized. We, therefore, recommend that you pursue the following scoring approach as well.

Summary Scores Compared to Adult Norms

Instead of just counting symptoms (items that are answered 2 or 3), in this approach you add up the total score the individual achieves for each of the three symptom lists (inattention, hyperactive–impulsive, ODD) across all the items that are answered on that list. In other words, sum all items answered 1, 2, or 3. Now compare the summary scores on each list to the accompanying table of norms from our region for your client's age group. Once again, use the score indicated in the column marked +1.5 *SD* as an indication of clinical significance.

You may find that adults who do not necessarily meet the DSM-IV recommended threshold used in the first approach do meet or exceed either of the clinically significant thresholds shown in the second or third approaches.

Scoring the Childhood Symptoms Scale—Self-Report Form

Follow the same three scoring approaches previously recommended for this scale as well. The results will tell you whether the client meets or exceeds the clinically significant thresholds by any of these approaches for their retrospective recall of their childhood years (ages 5–12 years). Remember that the diagnosis of ADHD requires not only that

Means, Standard Deviations, and Deviance Thresholds (+1.5 *SD*) by Age Group for the ADHD and ODD Summary Scores for Current Symptoms Collapsed across Gender

Symptom	Age (in years)	Mean	SD	+1.5 *SD* cuttoff	N
Inattention	17–29	6.3	4.7	13.4	275
Inattention	30–49	5.5	4.4	12.1	316
Inattention	50+	4.5	3.3	9.5	90
Hyper.–Impulsive	17–29	8.5	4.7	15.6	276
Hyper.–Impulsive	30–49	6.7	4.3	13.2	309
Hyper.–Impulsive	50+	5.1	3.2	9.9	93
Total ADHD score	17–29	14.7	8.7	27.8	266
Total ADHD score	30–49	12.0	7.8	23.7	299
Total ADHD score	50+	9.5	5.8	18.2	87
ODD score	17–29	6.1	4.7	13.2	271
ODD score	30–49	4.4	3.9	10.3	308
ODD score	50+	3.1	2.9	7.5	91

Note. N, sample size; *SD*, standard deviation.

clients have clinically significant (developmentally inappropriate) levels of current symptoms of ADHD but that they also have had clinically significant symptoms in childhood. That is the purpose of this second scale—to assist in determining whether developmentally inappropriate symptoms may have been present in childhood, at least according to the client's self-report.

The accompanying tables present the norms for our geographic region for the second (symptom counts compared to norms) and third (summary scores compared to norms) scoring approaches discussed previously as applied to the childhood recall form of this rating scale. Notice here that norms for males and females are provided separately within the tables. This is done because the study from which these data are derived found significant gender differences in the recall of symptoms in childhood, even though no such differences were significant in reporting current symptoms.

Scoring the Current and Childhood Symptoms Scale—Other Report Forms

These two scales are completed by someone who has known the client well, either currently (for Current Symptoms Scale) or as a child (for Childhood Symptoms Scale). We have not collected norms for these scales as completed by others about a client. And so the only scoring approach possible here is the first approach described above (symptom count compared to DSM-IV thresholds). Bear in mind that the same problem may plague this scoring approach for these scales as it did for the self-report forms of these scales; the DSM-IV thresholds may be excessively restrictive (too conservative) when applied to adults. In any case, use these scales mainly to obtain corroborative information about the presence and degree of ADHD symptoms experienced by the client at these two points in time.

Means, Standard Deviations, and Deviance Thresholds (+1.5 SD) by Age Group and Gender for the Positive Symptom Counts for the ADHD and ODD Symptom Lists for Retrospective Recall of Childhood Symptoms

Symptom	Age (in years)	Males				Females			
		Mean	SD	+1.5 SD	N	Mean	SD	+1.5 SD	N
Inattention	17–29	3.3	2.8	7.5	175	1.9	2.7	6.0	99
Inattention	30–49	2.2	2.5	6.0	182	1.7	2.6	5.6	133
Inattention	50+	0.7	1.4	2.8	55	0.2	0.7	1.3	38
Hyper.–Impulsive	17–29	3.1	2.7	7.2	174	2.5	2.5	6.3	100
Hyper.–Impulsive	30–49	2.2	2.5	6.0	181	1.4	2.0	4.4	135
Hyper.–Impulsive	50+	0.9	1.5	3.2	55	0.4	0.8	1.6	39
Total ADHD score	17–29	6.4	5.1	14.1	173	4.5	4.9	11.9	96
Total ADHD score	30–49	4.4	4.7	11.5	177	3.1	4.3	9.6	129
Total ADHD score	50+	1.6	2.2	4.9	54	0.5	1.1	2.2	37
ODD score	17–29	2.8	2.7	6.9	171	1.9	2.4	5.5	102
ODD score	30–49	1.6	2.4	5.2	178	1.0	2.0	4.0	133
ODD score	50+	0.5	1.2	2.3	54	0.2	1.0	1.7	39

Note. N, sample size; SD, standard deviation.

Means, Standard Deviations, and Deviance Thresholds (+1.5 SD) by Age Group and Gender for the ADHD and ODD Summary Scores for Retrospective Recall of Childhood Symptoms

Symptom	Age (in years)	Males				Females			
		Mean	SD	+1.5 SD	N	Mean	SD	+1.5 SD	N
Inattention	17–29	11.1	6.0	20.1	175	8.2	5.9	17.1	99
Inattention	30–49	8.9	5.6	17.3	182	7.2	6.1	16.4	133
Inattention	50+	6.1	4.0	12.1	55	3.5	3.1	8.2	38
Hyper.–Impulsive	17–29	10.7	6.0	19.7	174	9.0	6.0	18.0	100
Hyper.–Impulsive	30–49	8.4	5.6	16.8	181	6.0	5.1	13.7	135
Hyper.–Impulsive	50+	5.6	3.4	10.7	55	3.3	2.7	7.4	39
Total ADHD score	17–29	21.8	11.3	38.8	173	17.3	11.4	34.4	96
Total ADHD score	30–49	17.3	10.4	32.9	177	13.2	10.8	29.4	129
Total ADHD score	50+	11.6	6.2	20.9	54	6.3	4.5	13.1	37
ODD score	17–29	9.3	6.1	18.5	171	7.2	5.9	16.1	102
ODD score	30–49	6.9	5.5	15.2	178	4.8	4.9	12.2	133
ODD score	50+	3.9	3.6	9.3	54	2.4	3.1	7.1	39

Note. N, sample size; SD, standard deviation.

Reference

Murphy, K., & Barkley, R. A. (1996). Prevalence of DSM-IV ADHD symptoms in an adult community sample of licensed drivers. *Journal of Attention Disorders*, *1*, 147–161.

DEVELOPMENTAL HISTORY

Name_____ Date_____

1. As far as you know, were there any problems with your mother's   Yes   No
   pregnancy with you?
   If yes, please give details:

2. Were there any problems associated with her delivery of you?   Yes   No
   If yes, please give details:

3. Did your mother use alcohol or other drugs during the pregnancy?   Yes   No
   If yes, please give details:

4. Did your mother smoke cigarettes during the pregnancy?   Yes   No
   If yes, please give any details:

5. Did you have any significant delays in your development   Yes   No
   (i.e., in walking, talking, or sitting up)?
   If yes, please give details:

6. Did you have any serious childhood illnesses/diseases/   Yes   No
   major surgeries?
   If yes, please give details:

(cont.)

From *Attention-Deficit Hyperactivity Disorder: A Clinical Workbook* (2nd ed.) by Russell A. Barkley and Kevin R. Murphy. Copyright 1998 by The Guilford Press. Permission to photocopy this form is granted to purchasers of the *Workbook* for personal use only (see copyright page for details).

7. Did you have any problems getting along with other children   Yes   No
   when you were a child?
   If yes, please give details:

8. Please place a checkmark beside any of the following that you believe you had significant
   difficulties with as a child:

   _____ Defiant   _____ Aggressive   _____ Stubborn   _____ Destructive

   _____ Hyperactive   _____ Impulsive   _____ Inattentive   _____ Distractible

   _____ Shy   _____ Withdrawn   _____ Depressed   _____ Anxious

   _____ Fearful   _____ Lying   _____ Stealing   _____ Fighting

   _____ Learning   _____ Language   _____ Memory   _____ Motor skills

   _____ Sleeping   _____ Eating   _____ Toilet training

   _____ Strange ideas (explain):

   _____ Strange behavior (explain):

EMPLOYMENT HISTORY

Name_____ **Date**_____

1. What is your current employment status (circle one)?
   a. Full time   c. Unemployed   e. Homemaker
   b. Part time   d. Student   f. Disabled
2. What is your current occupation?_____
3. Who is your current employer?_____
4. How long have your worked in your present job?_____ years
5. Please give us your history of previous employment since completing your education:

Job title	Time on job (years)	Reason for leaving

6. What is your longest period of employment at one place?_____
7. Have you ever been fired from a job?   Yes   No
   If yes, how many jobs were you fired from or asked to leave by your
   employer?_____
8. Have you served in the military?   Yes   No
   If yes, please give details:

9. Briefly describe the types of problems you have experienced with work either at your
   current job or in the past:

From *Attention-Deficit Hyperactivity Disorder: A Clinical Workbook* (2nd ed.) by Russell A. Barkley and Kevin R. Murphy. Copyright 1998 by The Guilford Press. Permission to photocopy this form is granted to purchasers of the *Workbook* for personal use only (see copyright page for details).

HEALTH HISTORY

Name_____ **Date**_____

Have you ever had any of the following:

Type of problem	During childhood	Past as an adult	Currently
Allergies/asthma			
Heart problems			
Epilepsy or seizures			
High blood pressure			
Serious head injury			
Injury resulting in loss of consciousness			
Lead poisoning			
Broken bones			
Surgery			
Migraine headaches			
Thyroid condition			
Problems with vision			
Problems with hearing			
Diabetes			

Any other serious medical problems: (explain):

_____

Are you currently taking any medications?   Yes   No

If yes, please give details:

_____

Please describe any other health difficulties you have experienced now or in the past:

_____

From *Attention-Deficit Hyperactivity Disorder: A Clinical Workbook* (2nd ed.) by Russell A. Barkley and Kevin R. Murphy. Copyright 1998 by The Guilford Press. Permission to photocopy this form is granted to purchasers of the *Workbook* for personal use only (see copyright page for details).

SOCIAL HISTORY

Name_____ Date_____

1. How would you describe your mood most of the time? (circle one)
   a. Cheerful/happy   b. Sad/depressed   c. Changes all the time
   d. Anxious/nervous   e. Angry/irritable   d. Bland/unfeeling
2. Do your moods change *very* frequently, abruptly, and/or unpredictably?   Yes   No
   If yes, please give details:

3. Do you have trouble making friends?   Yes   No
4. Do you have trouble keeping friends?   Yes   No
5. Do you have trouble in your relationships with others?   Yes   No
   If yes, please give details:

6. Do you have problems with your temper?   Yes   No
   If yes, please give details:

7. Do you have a driver's license?   Yes   No
8. Has your license ever been suspended?   Yes   No
   If so, please explain why:

9. How many speeding tickets have you ever gotten?_____
10. Have you ever been stopped for driving while intoxicated?   Yes   No
    If so, how many times?_____ Were you arrested?   Yes   No
11. How many car accidents, regardless of fault, have you ever been involved in? _____
12. How many times did your family move during your childhood and adolescent years?_____
13. How many times have you moved since leaving high school?_____
14. If you believe that you have attention deficit hyperactivity disorder, or ADHD, please tell us in what way have your ADHD symptoms interfered with your life?

15. In what ways have you tried to compensate for or cope with your deficits?

From *Attention-Deficit Hyperactivity Disorder: A Clinical Workbook* (2nd ed.) by Russell A. Barkley and Kevin R. Murphy. Copyright 1998 by The Guilford Press. Permission to photocopy this form is granted to purchasers of the *Workbook* for personal use only (see copyright page for details).

CURRENT SYMPTOMS SCALE—SELF-REPORT FORM

Name_____ Date_____

Instructions: Please circle the number next to each item that best describes your behavior *during the past 6 months.*

Items:	Never or rarely	Sometimes	Often	Very often
1. Fail to give close attention to details or make careless mistakes in my work	0	1	2	3
2. Fidget with hands or feet or squirm in seat	0	1	2	3
3. Have difficulty sustaining my attention in tasks or fun activities	0	1	2	3
4. Leave my seat in situations in which seating is expected	0	1	2	3
5. Don't listen when spoken to directly	0	1	2	3
6. Feel restless	0	1	2	3
7. Don't follow through on instructions and fail to finish work	0	1	2	3
8. Have difficulty engaging in leisure activities or doing fun things quietly	0	1	2	3
9. Have difficulty organizing tasks and activities	0	1	2	3
10. Feel "on the go" or "driven by a motor"	0	1	2	3
11. Avoid, dislike, or am reluctant to engage in work that requires sustained mental effort	0	1	2	3
12. Talk excessively	0	1	2	3
13. Lose things necessary for tasks or activities	0	1	2	3
14. Blurt out answers before questions have been completed	0	1	2	3
15. Am easily distracted	0	1	2	3
16. Have difficulty awaiting turn	0	1	2	3
17. Am forgetful in daily activities	0	1	2	3
18. Interrupt or intrude on others	0	1	2	3

(cont.)

From *Attention-Deficit Hyperactivity Disorder: A Clinical Workbook* (2nd ed.) by Russell A. Barkley and Kevin R. Murphy. Copyright 1998 by The Guilford Press. Permission to photocopy this form is granted to purchasers of the *Workbook* for personal use only (see copyright page for details).

How old were you when these problems with attention, impulsiveness, or hyperactivity first began to occur? _____ years old

To what extent do the problems you may have circled on the previous page interfere with your ability to function in each of these areas of life activities?

Areas:	Never or rarely	Sometimes	Often	Very often
In my home life with my immediate family	0	1	2	3
In my work or occupation	0	1	2	3
In my social interactions with others	0	1	2	3
In my activities or dealings in the community	0	1	2	3
In any educational activities	0	1	2	3
In my dating or marital relationship	0	1	2	3
In my management of my money	0	1	2	3
In my driving of a motor vehicle	0	1	2	3
In my leisure or recreational activities	0	1	2	3
In my management of my daily responsibilities	0	1	2	3

Instructions: Again, please circle the number next to each item that best describes your behavior *during the past 6 months.*

Items:	Never or rarely	Sometimes	Often	Very often
1. Lose temper	0	1	2	3
2. Argue	0	1	2	3
3. Actively defy or refuse to comply with requests or rules	0	1	2	3
4. Deliberately annoy people	0	1	2	3
5. Blame others for my mistakes or misbehavior	0	1	2	3
6. Am touchy or easily annoyed by others	0	1	2	3
7. Am angry or resentful	0	1	2	3
8. Am spiteful or vindictive	0	1	2	3

CHILDHOOD SYMPTOMS SCALE—SELF-REPORT FORM

Name_____ **Date**_____

Instructions: Please circle the number next to each item that best describes your behavior *when you were a child age 5 to 12 years.*

Items:	Never or rarely	Sometimes	Often	Very often
1. Failed to give close attention to details or made careless mistakes in my work	0	1	2	3
2. Fidgeted with hands or feet or squirmed in seat	0	1	2	3
3. Had difficulty sustaining my attention in tasks or fun activities	0	1	2	3
4. Left my seat in classroom or in other situations in which seating was expected	0	1	2	3
5. Didn't listen when spoken to directly	0	1	2	3
6. Felt restless	0	1	2	3
7. Didn't follow through on instructions and failed to finish work	0	1	2	3
8. Had difficulty engaging in leisure activities or doing fun things quietly	0	1	2	3
9. Had difficulty organizing tasks and activities	0	1	2	3
10. Felt "on the go" or "driven by a motor"	0	1	2	3
11. Avoided, disliked, or was reluctant to engage in work that required sustained mental effort	0	1	2	3
12. Talked excessively	0	1	2	3
13. Lost things necessary for tasks or activities	0	1	2	3
14. Blurted out answers before questions were completed	0	1	2	3
15. Was easily distracted	0	1	2	3
16. Had difficulty awaiting turn	0	1	2	3
17. Was forgetful in daily activities	0	1	2	3
18. Interrupted or intruded on others	0	1	2	3

(cont.)

From *Attention-Deficit Hyperactivity Disorder: A Clinical Workbook* (2nd ed.) by Russell A. Barkley and Kevin R. Murphy. Copyright 1998 by The Guilford Press. Permission to photocopy this form is granted to purchasers of the *Workbook* for personal use only (see copyright page for details).

To what extent did the problems you may have circled on the previous page interfere with your ability to function in each of these areas of life activities *when you were a child between 5 and 12 years of age?*

Areas:	Never or rarely	Sometimes	Often	Very often
In my home life with my immediate family	0	1	2	3
In my social interactions with other children	0	1	2	3
In my activities or dealings in the community	0	1	2	3
In school	0	1	2	3
In sports, clubs, or other organizations	0	1	2	3
In learning to take care of myself	0	1	2	3
In my play, leisure, or recreational activities	0	1	2	3
In my handling of my daily chores or other responsibilities	0	1	2	3

Instructions: Again, please circle the number next to each item that best describes your behavior *when you were a child age 5 to 12 years.*

Items:	Never or rarely	Sometimes	Often	Very often
1. Lost temper	0	1	2	3
2. Argued with adults	0	1	2	3
3. Actively defied or refused to comply with adults' requests or rules	0	1	2	3
4. Deliberately annoyed people	0	1	2	3
5. Blamed others for my mistakes or misbehavior	0	1	2	3
6. Was touchy or easily annoyed by others	0	1	2	3
7. Was angry or resentful	0	1	2	3
8. Was spiteful or vindictive	0	1	2	3

(cont.)

Instructions: Please indicate whether you engaged in any of the following *during the period between 5 and 18 years of age:*

1. Often bullied, threatened, or intimidated others	No	Yes
2. Often initiated physical fights	No	Yes
3. Used a weapon that can cause serious physical harm to others (e.g., a bat, brick, broken bottle, knife, or gun)	No	Yes
4. Was physically cruel to people	No	Yes
5. Was physically cruel to animals	No	Yes
6. Stole while confronting a victim (e.g., mugging, purse snatching, extortion, armed robbery)	No	Yes
7. Forced someone into sexual activity	No	Yes
8. Deliberately engaged in fire setting with the intention of causing serious damage	No	Yes
9. Deliberately destroyed others' property (other than by fire setting)	No	Yes
10. Broke into someone else's house, building, or car	No	Yes
11. Often lied to obtain goods or favors or to avoid obligations (i.e., "conned" others)	No	Yes
12. Stole items of nontrivial value without confronting a victim (e.g., shoplifting, but without breaking and entering; forgery)	No	Yes
13. Often stayed out at night despite parental prohibitions If so, at what age did this begin?_____	No	Yes
14. Ran away from home overnight at least twice while living in parents' home, foster care, or group home. If so, how many times?_____	No	Yes
15. Was often truant from school If so, at what age did this begin?_____	No	Yes

CURRENT SYMPTOMS SCALE—OTHER REPORT FORM

Your name_____ **Date**_____

Person to be rated by you_____

Your relationship to that person_____

Instructions: Please rate the person named above by circling the number next to each item that best describes this person's behavior *during the past 6 months.*

Items:	Never or rarely	Sometimes	Often	Very often
1. Fails to give close attention to details or makes careless mistakes in his/her work	0	1	2	3
2. Fidgets with hands or feet or squirms in seat	0	1	2	3
3. Has difficulty sustaining his/her attention in tasks or fun activities	0	1	2	3
4. Leaves his/her seat in situations in which seating is expected	0	1	2	3
5. Doesn't listen when spoken to directly	0	1	2	3
6. Seems restless	0	1	2	3
7. Doesn't follow through on instructions and fails to finish work	0	1	2	3
8. Has difficulty engaging in leisure activities or doing fun things quietly	0	1	2	3
9. Has difficulty organizing tasks and activities				
10. Seems to be "on the go" or "driven by a motor"	0	1	2	3
11. Avoids, dislikes, or is reluctant to engage in work that requires sustained mental effort	0	1	2	3
12. Talks excessively	0	1	2	3
13. Loses things necessary for tasks or activities	0	1	2	3
14. Blurts out answers before questions have been completed	0	1	2	3
15. Is easily distracted	0	1	2	3

(cont.)

From *Attention-Deficit Hyperactivity Disorder: A Clinical Workbook* (2nd ed.) by Russell A. Barkley and Kevin R. Murphy. Copyright 1998 by The Guilford Press. Permission to photocopy this form is granted to purchasers of the *Workbook* for personal use only (see copyright page for details).

16. Has difficulty awaiting turn	0	1	2	3
17. Is forgetful in daily activities	0	1	2	3
18. Interrupts or intrudes on others	0	1	2	3

19. If you indicated that this person experienced any of the problems on the first page, at what age did these problems develop: At approximately _____ years old

To what extent do the problems you may have circled on the previous page interfere with this person's ability to function in each of these areas of life activities?

Areas:	Never or rarely	Sometimes	Often	Very often
In his/her home life with the immediate family	0	1	2	3
In his/her work or occupation	0	1	2	3
In his/her social interactions with others	0	1	2	3
In his/her activities or dealings in the community	0	1	2	3
In any educational activities	0	1	2	3
In his/her dating or marital relationship	0	1	2	3
In his/her management of money	0	1	2	3
In his/her driving of a motor vehicle	0	1	2	3
In his/her leisure or recreational activities	0	1	2	3
In his/her management of daily responsibilities	0	1	2	3

CHILDHOOD SYMPTOMS SCALE—OTHER REPORT FORM

Your name_____ Date_____

Person to be rated by you_____

Your relationship to that person_____

Instructions: Please circle the number next to each item that best describes the behavior of the person being rated when he/she was *a child age 5 to 12 years.*

Items:	Never or rarely	Sometimes	Often	Very often
1. Failed to give close attention to details or made careless mistakes in his/her work	0	1	2	3
2. Fidgeted with hands or feet or squirmed in seat	0	1	2	3
3. Had difficulty sustaining his/her attention in tasks or fun activities	0	1	2	3
4. Left his/her seat in classroom or in other situations in which seating was expected	0	1	2	3
5. Didn't listen when spoken to directly	0	1	2	3
6. Seemed restless	0	1	2	3
7. Didn't follow through on instructions and failed to finish work	0	1	2	3
8. Had difficulty engaging in leisure activities or doing fun things quietly	0	1	2	3
9. Had difficulty organizing tasks and activities	0	1	2	3
10. Seemed "on the go" or "driven by a motor"	0	1	2	3
11. Avoided, disliked, or was reluctant to engage in work that required sustained mental effort	0	1	2	3
12. Talked excessively	0	1	2	3
13. Lost things necessary for tasks or activities	0	1	2	3
14. Blurted out answers before questions were completed	0	1	2	3
15. Was easily distracted	0	1	2	3
16. Had difficulty awaiting turn	0	1	2	3

(cont.)

From *Attention-Deficit Hyperactivity Disorder: A Clinical Workbook* (2nd ed.) by Russell A. Barkley and Kevin R. Murphy. Copyright 1998 by The Guilford Press. Permission to photocopy this form is granted to purchasers of the *Workbook* for personal use only (see copyright page for details).

	Never or rarely	Sometimes	Often	Very often
17. Was forgetful in daily activities	0	1	2	3
18. Interrupted or intruded on others	0	1	2	3

To what extent did the problems you may have circled on the previous page interfere with this person's ability to function in each of these areas of life activities *when he/she was a child between 5 and 12 years of age?*

Areas:	Never or rarely	Sometimes	Often	Very often
In his/her home life with the immediate family	0	1	2	3
In his/her social interactions with other children	0	1	2	3
In his/her activities or dealings in the community	0	1	2	3
In school	0	1	2	3
In sports, clubs, or other organizations	0	1	2	3
In learning to take care of him/herself	0	1	2	3
In his/her play, leisure, or recreational activities	0	1	2	3
In his/her handling of daily chores or other responsibilities	0	1	2	3

Instructions: Again, please circle the number next to each item that best describes the behavior of the person being rated *when he/she was a child age 5 to 12 years.*

Items:	Never or rarely	Sometimes	Often	Very often
1. Lost temper	0	1	2	3
2. Argued with adults	0	1	2	3
3. Actively defied or refused to comply with adults' requests or rules	0	1	2	3
4. Deliberately annoyed people	0	1	2	3
5. Blamed others for his/her mistakes or misbehavior	0	1	2	3
6. Was touchy or easily annoyed by others	0	1	2	3
7. Was angry or resentful	0	1	2	3
8. Was spiteful or vindictive	0	1	2	3

(cont.)

Instructions: Please indicate whether the person being rated on this form engaged in any of the following items *between 5 and 18 years of age:*

1. Often bullied, threatened, or intimidated others	No	Yes
2. Often initiated physical fights	No	Yes
3. Used a weapon that can cause serious physical harm to others (e.g., a bat, brick, broken bottle, knife, or gun)	No	Yes
4. Was physically cruel to people	No	Yes
5. Was physically cruel to animals	No	Yes
6. Stole while confronting a victim (e.g., mugging, purse snatching, extortion, armed robbery)	No	Yes
7. Forced someone into sexual activity	No	Yes
8. Deliberately engaged in fire setting with the intention of causing serious damage	No	Yes
9. Deliberately destroyed others' property (other than by fire setting)	No	Yes
10. Broke into someone else's house, building, or car	No	Yes
11. Often lied to obtain goods or favors or to avoid obligations (i.e., "conned" others)	No	Yes
12. Stole items of nontrivial value without confronting a victim (e.g., shoplifting, but without breaking and entering; forgery)	No	Yes
13. Often stayed out at night despite parental prohibitions If so, at what age did this begin?_____	No	Yes
14. Ran away from home overnight at least twice while living in parents' home, foster care, or group home. If so, how many times?_____	No	Yes
15. Was often truant from school If so, at what age did this begin?_____	No	Yes

CHILDHOOD SCHOOL PERFORMANCE SCALE—OTHER REPORT FORM

Your name_____ Date_____

Person to be rated by you_____

Your relationship to that person _____

Instructions: Please think back to when the person named above ("person to be rated") was a child in school. We want you to tell us about their behavior at school and their typical school performance. Please circle the number next to each item that best describes the behavior of this person in school *when he/she was in grades 1 to 12.*

Items:	Never or rarely	Sometimes	Often	Very often
1. Failed to give close attention to details or made careless mistakes in his/her work	0	1	2	3
2. Fidgeted with hands or feet or squirmed in seat	0	1	2	3
3. Had difficulty sustaining his/her attention in tasks or fun activities	0	1	2	3
4. Left his/her seat in classroom or in other situations in which seating was expected	0	1	2	3
5. Didn't listen when spoken to directly	0	1	2	3
6. Seemed restless	0	1	2	3
7. Didn't follow through on instructions and failed to finish work	0	1	2	3
8. Had difficulty engaging in leisure activities or doing fun things quietly	0	1	2	3
9. Had difficulty organizing tasks and activities	0	1	2	3
10. Seemed "on the go" or "driven by a motor"	0	1	2	3
11. Avoided, disliked, or was reluctant to engage in work that required sustained mental effort	0	1	2	3
12. Talked excessively	0	1	2	3
13. Lost things necessary for tasks or activities	0	1	2	3

(cont.)

From *Attention-Deficit Hyperactivity Disorder: A Clinical Workbook* (2nd ed.) by Russell A. Barkley and Kevin R. Murphy. Copyright 1998 by The Guilford Press. Permission to photocopy this form is granted to purchasers of the *Workbook* for personal use only (see copyright page for details).

14. Blurted out answers before questions had been completed	0	1	2	3
15. Was easily distracted	0	1	2	3
16. Had difficulty awaiting turn	0	1	2	3
17. Was forgetful in daily activities	0	1	2	3
18. Interrupted or intruded on others	0	1	2	3

To what extent did this person have difficulties in the following areas of school performance when he/she were in grades 1 to 12?

Areas:	Never or rarely	Sometimes	Often	Very often
In his/her completion of classwork	0	1	2	3
In his/her completion of homework assignments	0	1	2	3
In his/her behavior in the school classroom	0	1	2	3
In his/her behavior on the school bus	0	1	2	3
In sports, clubs, or other organizations held at school	0	1	2	3
In his/her interactions with classmates	0	1	2	3
In his/her play or recreational activities at recess	0	1	2	3
In his/her behavior in the lunchroom at school	0	1	2	3
In his/her management of time at school	0	1	2	3

1. Was this person ever held back a grade in school?	Yes	No
2. Was this person ever suspended or expelled from school?	Yes	No
3. Did this person receive any special education services?	Yes	No
4. Was this person punished at school more often than others?	Yes	No
5. Did this person skip school without permission?	Yes	No
6. Did this person drop out or fail to graduate high school?	Yes	No
7. Did this person ever take any medication to help manage his/her behavior at school?	Yes	No

WORK PERFORMANCE RATING SCALE—SELF-REPORT FORM

Name_____ **Date**_____

Instructions: Please rate yourself in your own work performance by circling the number next to each item that best describes your behavior at work *during the past 6 months.*

Items:	Never or rarely	Sometimes	Often	Very often
1. Fail to give close attention to details or make careless mistakes in my work	0	1	2	3
2. Fidget with hands or feet or squirm in seat	0	1	2	3
3. Have difficulty sustaining attention in tasks or other work-related activities	0	1	2	3
4. Leave my seat in meetings, classes, or in other situations in which seating is expected	0	1	2	3
5. Do not listen when spoken to directly	0	1	2	3
6. Feel restless	0	1	2	3
7. Do not follow through on instructions and fail to finish work	0	1	2	3
8. Have difficulty working quietly	0	1	2	3
9. Have difficulty organizing tasks and activities	0	1	2	3
10. Seem to be "on the go" or "driven by a motor"	0	1	2	3
11. Avoid, dislike, or am reluctant to engage in work that requires sustained mental effort	0 / 0	1 / 1	2 / 2	3 / 3
12. Talk excessively	0	1	2	3
13. Lose things necessary for tasks or activities	0	1	2	3
14. Blurt out answers before questions have been completed	0	1	2	3
15. Am easily distracted	0	1	2	3
16. Have difficulty awaiting turn in group activities	0	1	2	3
17. Am forgetful in daily activities	0	1	2	3
18. Interrupt or intrude on others	0	1	2	3

(cont.)

From *Attention-Deficit Hyperactivity Disorder: A Clinical Workbook* (2nd ed.) by Russell A. Barkley and Kevin R. Murphy. Copyright 1998 by The Guilford Press. Permission to photocopy this form is granted to purchasers of the *Workbook* for personal use only (see copyright page for details).

To what extent do the problems you may have circled on the previous page interfere with your ability to function in each of these areas of work activities?

Areas:	Never or rarely	Sometimes	Often	Very often
In my interactions with my coworkers	0	1	2	3
In my performance of assigned work	0	1	2	3
In my interactions with supervisors	0	1	2	3
In my activities or dealings with clients, customers, or the general public	0	1	2	3
In any educational activities at work	0	1	2	3
In my punctuality for work	0	1	2	3
In my management of my time and work-related deadlines	0	1	2	3
In my operation of any work-related equipment	0	1	2	3
In my operation of any work-related motor vehicles	0	1	2	3
In my management of my daily responsibilities	0	1	2	3

In general, how would you rate your overall work performance and productivity as an employee? (circle one)

1. Excellent   2. Above average   3. Average   4. Below average   5. Poor

ADULT INTERVIEW

Client's name_____ **Date**_____

Date of birth_____ Age_____ Clinic record #_____

Marital status: [*Circle one*]   Single   Married   Divorced   Separated   Widowed

Ethnic group_____

Primary referral source: [*Circle one only*]

   1. Self   5. Child ADHD clinic

   2. Parent   6. Friend

   3. Physician   7. Other_____

   4. Mental health professional

Participants in this interview: [*Check all that apply*]

   Patient_____   Spouse ____   Mother____   Father _____   Sibling _____

   Friend _____   Other _____

Reason for referral:

Goals/purposes of evaluation:

LEGAL DISCLOSURES

[*Interviewer, as part of the interview, be certain to review any necessary legal disclosures pertinent to your state, country, or other geographic region. For instance, in Massachusetts, we advise clients of the following four issues:*

   1. *Any disclosure of information that indicates a suspicion of child abuse must be reported to state authorities (Department of Social Services).*
   2. *Any disclosure of current threats of harm to oneself, as in a specific suicide threat, will result in immediate referral to an emergency mental health unit.*
   3. *Any disclose of specific current threats to specific individuals will result in notification of those individuals concerning the threat.*
   4. *Although the mental health records are confidential, they may be subpoenaed by a judge's order and must be provided to the court if so ordered.*

Take time now to cover any such issues with the client before proceeding to the remainder of this interview.]

(cont.)

From *Attention-Deficit Hyperactivity Disorder: A Clinical Workbook* (2nd ed.) by Russell A. Barkley and Kevin R. Murphy. Copyright 1998 by The Guilford Press. Permission to photocopy this form is granted to purchasers of the *Workbook* for personal use only (see copyright page for details).

Please provide a brief description of your major concerns presently:

When would you say these symptoms began?

1. 0–7 years
2. 8–12 years
3. 13–15 years

4. 16–21 years
5. 22 years to present

Please describe briefly the history of these concerns and provide some highlights as to how they have affected you during your life:

REVIEW OF ADHD SYMPTOMS

[Interviewer: In this section, please review with the client his/her self-reports of the ADI ID symptom list. If a parent or someone who knows the client well since childhood has accompanied the client to the interview, please record his/her impression of the client's ADHD symptoms currently and in childhood. Otherwise, this information can be obtained later by telephone interview with the parent or other person. Simply use the columns next to each symptom to record the answers paying attention to the fact that you are inquiring both about the presence of the symptom now and whether or not it was present in childhood, ages 5–12 years. Place a "1" in the column next to each symptom if that symptom is or was present to a developmentally inappropriate degree. Use a "0" if the symptom was not present or did not occur to an inappropriate degree.]

Instructions: Please tell me whether or not you have experienced any of the following behaviors to a degree that would be considered significant or developmentally inappropriate for your age *during the past 6 months*. I will then ask you if you also experienced this behavior to an inappropriate degree *when you were a child between the ages of 5 and 12 years.*

(cont.)

Items:	Client self-report		Parent/other	
	Now	5–12	Now	5–12
1. Failed to give close attention to details or made careless mistakes in your work				
2. Fidgeted with hands or feet or squirmed in seat				
3. Had difficulty sustaining your attention in tasks or fun activities				
4. Left your seat in situations in which seating is expected				
5. Didn't listen when spoken to directly				
6. Felt restless				
7. Didn't follow through on instructions and failed to finish work				
8. Had difficulty engaging in leisure activities or doing fun things quietly				
9. Had difficulty organizing tasks and activities				
10. Felt "on the go" or "driven by a motor"				
11. Avoided, disliked, or were reluctant to engage in work that required sustained mental effort				
12. Talked excessively				
13. Lost things necessary for tasks or activities				
14. Blurted out answers before questions were completed				
15. Were easily distracted				
16. Had difficulty awaiting turn				
17. Were forgetful in daily activities				
18. Interrupted or intruded on others				

Approximately how old were you when these problems with attention, impulsiveness, or hyperactivity first began to occur? _____ years old

[Interviewer: Record here the total number of inattention symptoms, items 1–9, and hyperactive–impulsive symptoms, items 10–18, reported by the client as well as by the parent or other person you have interviewed about these symptoms for both current functioning and childhood functioning.

(cont.)

Diagnostic criteria require at least 6 of 9 inattention symptoms or 6 of 9 hyperactive–impulsive symptoms are currently present and that the disorder was present in childhood.]

	Self-reported ADHD symptoms	Parent/other-reported ADHD symptoms
Current Inattention	_____	_____
Current Hyperactivity–Impulsivity	_____	_____
Childhood Inattention	_____	_____
Childhood Hyperactivity–Impulsivity	_____	_____

Do the problems you have reported from this list of behaviors interfere with or impair your ability to function in each of these areas of life activities to a significant degree?

Areas:	Client self-report		Parent/other	
	Now	5–12	Now	5–12
In your home life with your immediate family				
In your work or occupation				
In your social interactions with others				
In your activities or dealings in the community				
In any educational activities				
In your dating or marital relationships				
In your management of money				
In your driving of a motor vehicle				
In your leisure or recreational activities				
In your management of daily responsibilities				

If the answer to any of the above is yes, please provide me with some brief details of how these areas of functioning have been impaired by your symptoms:

Besides the things I have just reviewed with you, do you have any difficulties in any other areas of your daily functioning?:

(cont.)

Do you experience any problems with the following: (1= Yes; 0 = No)

	Client	Parent/other
Making decisions or taking action too quickly		
Inconsistent work performance		
Low self-esteem; feeling demoralized		
Hot-tempered		
Daydream a lot		
Procrastinate often		
Rebellious, disobedient, or sassy		
Have few close friends		
Have difficulties with maintaining intimate relationships		
School performance substantially below your academic and intellectual potential		
Poor sense of time		
Trouble with authorities, teachers; labeled a discipline problem		
Bored often or easily		
Chronic pattern of underachievement		
Work best when under pressure or imminent deadline		
Consider yourself lazy		

Did your parents ever take you to see anyone about these problems when you were a child or adolescent?   Yes   No   If yes, please give me some brief details:

Did your parents complain that you were difficult to manage or control as a child?   Yes   No
If yes, please give me some brief details about this problem:

(cont.)

BEHAVIOR/CONDUCT DIFFICULTIES

Symptoms of Oppositional Defiant Disorder

[Interviewer: Review with the client whether or not he/she is currently experiencing any of the following behavioral difficulties to a degree that is inappropriate for his/her age and whether or not he/she recalls experiencing any in childhood that were inappropriate for his/her age. Criteria are four or more with onset during childhood years.]

Instructions: Please tell me if you have experienced any difficulties in the following areas of behavior *during the past 6 months*. I am also going to ask you if you experienced any difficulties with these same behaviors *as a child, ages 5–12 years*. In both cases, I want to know if these difficulties occurred to a degree that was inappropriate for that age period.

Behaviors:	Now	Ages 5–12
1. Lost temper		
2. Argued with others		
3. Actively defied or refused to comply with others' requests or rules		
4. Deliberately annoyed people		
5. Blamed others for your mistakes or misbehavior		
6. Were touchy or easily annoyed by others		
7. Were angry or resentful		
8. Were spiteful or vindictive		

At what age did these behavioral difficulties first develop?_____

Conduct Disorder (Childhood/Adolescence)

[Interviewer: Review with the client whether or not he/she engaged in any of the following activities prior to 18 years of age. Diagnostic criteria: 3 or more, duration > 6 months. Answer all items: Enter 1 if present, 0 if absent.]

Aggression to People and Animals

1. Often bullied, threatened, or intimidated others _____
2. Often initiated physical fights _____
3. Used a weapon that can cause serious physical harm to others _____
4. Were physically cruel to people _____
5. Were physically cruel to animals _____
6. Stole while confronting a victim (e.g., mugging, purse snatching, armed robbery) _____
7. Forced someone into sexual activity _____

(cont.)

Destruction of Property

8. Deliberately engaged in fire setting with the intention of causing serious damage _____
9. Deliberately destroyed others' property _____

Deceitfulness or Theft

10. Broke into someone else's house, building, or car _____
11. Often lied _____
11. Stole items of nontrivial value without confronting a victim (e.g., shoplifting) _____

Serious Violations of Rules

13. Often stayed out at night despite parental prohibitions, beginning before age 13 years _____
14. Ran away from home overnight at least twice _____
15. Were often truant from school, beginning before age 13 years _____

Total _____
Age of onset _____

[If client meets criteria for Conduct Disorder, administer interview items for Antisocial Personality Disorder; otherwise, not applicable.]

Antisocial Personality Disorder

Were you ever arrested or in trouble with the law? [Yes = 1, No = 0] _____
Details:

[Interviewer: Inquire of the client whether or not he/she has engaged in any of the following activities currently or since 18 years of age. Diagnostic criteria: Presence of Conduct Disorder before age 18 years and at least 3 of the following: Yes = 1, No = 0.]

	Client	Parent/ other
1. Failed to conform to social norms with respect to lawful behaviors as indicated by repeatedly performing acts that are grounds for arrest		
2. Were deceitful, as indicated by repeated lying, use of aliases, or conning others for personal profit or pleasure		
3. Were impulsive or failed to plan ahead		
4. Were irritable and aggressive, as indicated by repeated physical fights or assaults		
5. Showed reckless disregard for safety of self or others		

(cont.)

6. Demonstrated consistent irresponsibility, as indicated by repeated
   failure to sustain consistent work behavior or honor financial obligations

7. Showed lack of remorse, as indicated by being indifferent
   to or rationalizing having hurt, mistreated, or stolen from another

FAMILY HISTORY

If married, length of current marriage _____ Number of times married _____

Spouse's occupation _____ Spouse's education (years)_____

Number of children _____ Their ages _____

Number of siblings _____Their ages _____

Parents' marital status: 1 = married, 2 = divorced, 3 = widowed, 4 = separated, 5 = both
   deceased _____

Father's occupation _____ Father's education _____

Mother's occupation_____ Mother's education_____

Briefly describe for me what growing up in your family was like:

PAST PSYCHIATRIC HISTORY

(Yes = 1, No = 0)

Have you been previously diagnosed with ADHD?   ____

Are you currently seeing a therapist or psychiatrist?   ____
   Details:

Have you ever seen a counselor or psychiatrist before?   ____
   Details:

Have you ever been hospitalized for a psychiatric problem?   ____
   Details:

(cont.)

Have you ever had problems with depression?
Details:

_____

Have you ever had any suicidal thoughts?
Details:

_____

Have you ever made any suicide attempts?
Details:

_____

Number of suicide attempts:

_____

Have you ever had problems with anxiety?
Details:

_____

Have you ever had any problems with alcohol/drug abuse?
Details:

_____

Have you ever been treated for alcohol/drug problems?
Details:

_____

How much alcohol do you drink per week?
    1. I never drink   2. 0–1 drink   3. 2–4 drinks
    4. 5–10 drinks   5. > 10

_____

Are you using any other drugs recreationally presently?

_____

    If yes, which ones?

    a. Marijuana, hashish

_____

    b. Amphetamines, speed

_____

    c. Barbiturates, sleeping pills, quaaludes

_____

    d. Tranquilizers, Valium, Librium

_____

    e. Cocaine

_____

(cont.)

    f. Heroin   ____

    g. Opiates, morphine, Demerol   ____

    h. Psychedelics (LSD, Mescaline)   ____

    i. Other   ____

Have you ever been on any psychotropic medications?   ____
    Details:

OTHER CONCERNS

(Yes = 1; No = 0)

Areas:	Past	Present
Prolonged periods of sadness/depression		
Excessive anxiety		
Excessive fears, phobias		
Panic or anxiety attacks		
Obsessions/preoccupations		
Compulsions/compulsive habits or rituals		
Delusions		
Hallucinations		
Significant appetite changes		
Significant changes to sleep pattern		
Manic episodes		

Other symptoms of mental distress (explain):

[Interviewer: Note that if any of the above were checked as occurring either in the past or in the present, you may want to review the DSM-IV criteria for these respective disorders with the client to determine whether he/she meets diagnostic criteria for any of these disorders. The diagnostic criteria for those disorders most commonly associated with clinic-referred adults with ADHD are provided below.]

(cont.)

ANXIETY AND MOOD DISORDERS

Now I would like to ask you some questions about your emotions in general and your emotional reactions to some specific situations. I'll begin by asking you about any specific fears that you may have. Then I will ask you about your general mood or emotional condition throughout much of the day. Let's start with some specific fears that you may have.

Specific Phobia

[*Interviewer: Diagnosis requires that all criteria A through E be met.*]

A. Do you show a marked and persistent fear that is excessive or unreasonable in response to the presence of or the anticipation of a specific object or situation? For instance, in response to or anticipation of certain animals, heights, being in the dark, thunder storms or lightning, flying, receiving an injection, seeing blood, or any other things or situations? [*Enter 1 if yes, 0 if no, and ? if unknown.*] ____

[*Interviewer: If A is Yes, answer the following and proceed to B through G; otherwise, skip to next disorder. If any of criteria B–E are not met, skip to the next disorder.*]

What specifically are you fearful of?_____

B. Do you have this anxious or fearful reaction almost invariably when exposed to [specific thing or situation]? [*Enter 1 if yes, 0 if no, and ? if unknown.*] ____

[*Interviewer: This may include a panic attack in the presence of the feared object, thing, or situation, or anxiety expressed by crying, tantrums, freezing, or clinging.*]

C. Do you attempt to avoid this thing or situation or, if you must be exposed to it, do you endure it with intense anxiety or distress? [*Enter 1 if yes, 0 if no, and ? if unknown.*] ____

D. Do you avoid, fear anticipation of, or have an anxious reaction to this thing or situation that interferes significantly with any of the following? [*Enter 1 if yes, 0 if no, and ? if unknown; only one of these conditions needs to be endorsed for this criterion to be met.*]

Your normal routine_____   Academic or occupational functioning_____

Social activities_____   Social relationships_____

Does your having this fear cause you marked distress? ____

E. Have you had this fearful or anxious reaction to this thing or event vfor at least the past 6 months? [*Enter 1 if yes, 0 if no, and ? if unknown*] ____

F. Exclusion Criteria: [*Interviewer: Enter 1 if this phobia or anxiety is better accounted for by another mental disorder, such as Obsessive–Compulsive Disorder, Posttraumatic Stress Disorder, Separation Anxiety Disorder, Social Phobia, or Panic Disorder. Enter 0 if not and ? if unknown.*]

(cont.)

Diagnostic Code

Requirements for diagnosis:

Does each section A through E equal 1 or more? ____
Does section F total 0? ____

[*Check here if all requirements are met.*]

☐ Specific Phobia (300.29)

Social Phobia

[*Interviewer: Diagnosis requires that all criteria A through F be met, but the person must have developed the capacity for age-appropriate social relationships with familiar people and the anxiety must occur in interactions with others.*]

What about social situations?

A. [*Enter 1 if present, 0 if absent, and ? if unknown.*]

1. Do you show a marked and persistent fear that is excessive or unreasonable in response to the presence of or the anticipation of a social or performance situation in which you are exposed to unfamiliar people or to possible scrutiny by others? ____

2. Do you fear that you will act in a way that will be embarrassing or humiliating or be so anxious that it will be humiliating or embarrassing for you? ____

[*Interviewer: If parts 1 and 2 of A are present, answer the next question and proceed with remaining criteria below; otherwise skip to the next disorder. If any of the remaining criteria below are not met, skip to the next disorder.*]

3. What specific social situation are you fearful of? ____

B. Do you have this anxious or fearful reaction almost invariably when exposed to this situation? [*Enter 1 if present, 0 if absent, and ? if unknown.*] ____

[*Interviewer: This may include a panic attack in this social situation.*]

C. Do you attempt to avoid this situation or, if you must be exposed to it, do you endure it with intense anxiety or distress? [*Enter 1 if present, 0 if absent, and ? if unknown.*] ____

D. Do you show avoidance of, anticipation of, or anxious reaction to this situation such that it interferes significantly with any of the following? [*Enter 1 if present, 0 if absent, and ? if unknown.*] ____

[*Interviewer: Only one of these conditions needs to be endorsed for this criterion to be met.*]

Your normal routine_____   Academic or occupational functioning_____

Social activities_____   Social relationships_____

Does your having this fear cause you marked distress_____

(cont.)

E. Have you had this fearful or anxious reaction to this situation for at least the past 6 months. [*Enter 1 if present, 0 if absent, and ? if unknown.*] ____

F. Exclusion Criteria: [*Interviewer: Enter 1 if this phobia or anxiety is due to the direct physiological effects of a substance or a general medical condition or is better accounted for by another mental disorder, such as Panic Disorder, Separation Anxiety Disorder, Body Dysmorphic Disorder, Pervasive Developmental Disorder, or Schizoid Personality Disorder. If a general medical condition or another mental disorder is present, enter 1 if the fear in criterion A is related to it. Enter 0 if not, and ? if unknown.*]

Diagnostic Code

Requirements for diagnosis:

    Does section A total 2? ____
    Does each section B through E equal 1 or more? ____
    Does section F total 0 ____

[*Check here if all requirements are met.*]
    ☐ Social Phobia (300.23)
       Specify if Generalized (fear includes most social situations)

Generalized Anxiety Disorder

[*Interviewer: Diagnosis requires that each item in criteria A and B be met; that at least one symptom in criterion C be present for at least 6 months on more days than not; that symptoms produce clinically significant distress or impairment in social, academic, occupational, or other important areas of functioning; and that other disorders be excluded as indicated below.*]

Now let's talk about whether you generally tend to be anxious or to worry a lot compared to others.

A. [*Enter 1 if present, 0 if absent, and ? if unknown*]

   1. Do you show excessive anxiety and worry about a number of events or activities, such as work activities, school performance, or any other situations? [*Enter 1 if present, 0 if absent, and ? if unknown.*] ____

   2. Has this anxiety or worry occurred on more days than not for at least the last 6 months? [*Enter 1 if present, 0 if absent, and ? if unknown.*] ____

     [*Interviewer: If the questions in A were endorsed, proceed with remaining criteria for this disorder; otherwise, skip to next disorder. If any of the remaining criteria below are not met, skip to the next disorder.*]

B. Do you find it difficult to control your worry? [*Enter 1 if present, 0 if absent, and ? if unknown.*] ____

(cont.)

116

C. Generalized Anxiety Disorder Symptom List
   Has your anxiety or worry been associated with any of the following behaviors?
   [*Enter 1 if present, 0 if absent, and ? if unknown.*] ____

   [*Interviewer: Only one condition needs to be present for this criterion to be met.*]

   1. Restlessness or feeling keyed up or on edge ____

   2. Being easily fatigued or tired ____

   3. Difficulty concentrating or mind going blank ____

   4. Irritability ____

   5. Muscle tension ____

   6. Sleep disturbance or difficulties falling asleep, staying asleep, or restless
      and unsatisfying sleep ____

D. Have these worries created distress for you or impairment in any of the following areas?
   [*Enter 1 if present, 0 if absent, and ? if unknown.*]

   Social relations with others_____   Academic or occupational performance_____

   Any other areas of functioning_____   (explain) _____

E. Exclusion Criteria: [*Interviewer: Enter 1 if the anxiety or worry are confined to features of another mental disorder, such as being worried about having a panic attack (Panic Disorder), being contaminated (Obsessive Compulsive Disorder), being away from home or major attachment figures (Separation Anxiety Disorder), having multiple physical complaints (Somatization Disorder), or having a serious illness (Hypochondriasis), or the anxiety is associated with Posttraumatic Stress Disorder. Enter 0 if not and ? if unknown.*] ____

Diagnostic Code

Requirements for diagnosis:

   Does section A total 2? ____
   Does section B total 1? ____
   Does section C total 1 or more? ____
   Does section D total 1 or more? ____
   Does section E total 0? ____

[*Check here if all requirements are met.*]
   ☐ Generalized Anxiety Disorder (300.02)

Dysthymic Disorder

[*Interviewer: Diagnosis requires that depressed mood exist for most of the day, for more days than not, for at least 1 year; that at least two symptoms from section B exist; that the individual has never been without the symptoms in sections A and B for 2 consecutive months during the 1 year of the disturbance; that all exclusionary criteria are met; and the symptoms cause clinically significant distress or impairment in social, academic, or other important areas of functioning.*]

(cont.)

I would like to speak with you now about your mood as it occurs for most of the time.

A. [*Enter 1 if present, 0 if absent, and ? if unknown.*]

   1. Do you have depressed mood for most of the day?   ____

   2. Has this depressed mood occurred more days than not for at least the past 12 months?   ____

[*Interviewer: If the two questions in A were endorsed, proceed with remaining criteria for this disorder; otherwise skip to next disorder. If any of the remaining criteria are not met, skip to the next disorder.*]

B. Do you show any of the following difficulties while you are depressed: [*Enter 1 if present, 0 if absent, and ? if unknown.*]

   1. Poor appetite or overeating   ____

   2. Insomnia (trouble falling asleep) or hypersomnia (excessive sleeping)   ____

   3. Low energy or fatigue   ____

   4. Low self-esteem   ____

   5. Poor concentration or difficulty making decisions   ____

   6. Feelings of hopelessness   ____

C. During the 12 months or more that you have experienced this depressed mood, have you ever been without this depressed mood or the other difficulties you mentioned for at least two months? [*Enter 0 if client has had a 2-month remission, 1 if client has not had any remission of symptoms for at least 2 months, and ? if unknown.*]   ____

D. Has this depressed mood created distress for you or impairment in any of the following areas? [*Enter 1 if present, 0 if absent, and ? if unknown.*]   ____

Social relations with others_____   Academic or occupational performance_____

Any other areas of functioning_____ (explain)_____

E. Exclusion Criteria: [*Interviewer: Enter 1 if person meets criteria for Major Depressive Episode during the year or more of his/her mood disorder or if the disorder is better accounted for by Major Depressive Disorder. Also, enter 1 if there has ever been a manic episode, mixed manic–depressive episode, or hypomanic episode or if criteria for cyclothymic disorder apply. Enter 1 if the mood disorder described occurs exclusively during the course of a chronic psychosis, schizophrenia, or delusional disorder or is the result of the direct physiological effects of a substance or a general medical condition. Enter 0 if not and ? if unknown.*]

(cont.)

118

Diagnostic Code

Requirements for diagnosis:

Does section A total 2? ____
Does section B total 2? ____
Does section C total 1? ____
Does section D total 1 or more? ____
Does section E total 0? ____

[*Check here if all requirements are met.*]

☐ Dysthymic Disorder (300.4)

Major Depressive Episode

[*Interviewer: Diagnosis requires that at least five or more of the symptoms listed in A have been presented for a 2-week period; that this represents a change from previous functioning; that at least one of the symptoms is depressed mood or loss of interest or pleasure; that the symptoms create clinically significant distress or impairment in social, academic, or other important areas of functioning; and that all exclusion criteria are met.*]

Let's continue to talk about your mood or emotional adjustment. Have you experienced any of the following for at least a 2-week period?

A. Major Depressive Episode Symptom List: [*Enter 1 if present, 0 if absent, and ? if unknown.*]

1. Depressed or irritable mood most of the day nearly every day for at least 2 weeks ____

2. Markedly diminished interest or pleasure in all or almost all activities most of the day, nearly every day for at least 2 weeks ____

[*Interviewer: If either 1 or 2 was endorsed, proceed with remaining criteria; otherwise, skip to next disorder.*]

3. Significant weight loss when not dieting ____

Significant weight gain ____

Decrease or increase in appetite nearly every day ____

4. Insomnia (trouble falling asleep) or hypersomnia (excessive sleep) nearly every day ____

5. Agitated or excessive movement nearly every day ____

Or lethargic, sluggish, slow moving, or significantly reduced movement or activity nearly every day ____

6. Fatigue or loss of energy nearly every day ____

7. Feelings of worthlessness or excessive or inappropriate guilt nearly every day [*Interviewer: This should not just be self-reproach or guilt about being sick.*] ____

(*cont.*)

8. Diminished ability to think or concentrate, or indecisiveness, nearly every day ____

9. Recurrent thoughts of death ____

   Or recurrent thoughts of suicide without a specific plan ____

   Or suicide attempt or a specific plan for committing suicide ____

B. Have these symptoms of depression created distress for you or impairment in any of the following areas? [*Enter 1 if present, 0 if absent, and ? if unknown.*]

Social relations with others_____ Academic or occupational performance_____

Any other areas of functioning_____ (explain)_____

C. Exclusion Criteria: [*Interviewer: Enter 1 if person meets criteria for Manic–Depression, if the symptoms are due to direct physiological effects of a substance of a general medical condition, or if the symptoms are better accounted for by clinical bereavement after the loss of a loved one. Enter 0 if not and ? if unknown.*]

Diagnostic Code

Requirements for diagnosis:

> Do questions 1 and 2 in section A total 1 or more? ____
> Does section A total 5 or more? ____
> Does section B total 1 or more? ____
> Does section C total 0? ____

[*Check here if all requirements are met.*]

☐ Major Depressive Disorder (296.xx)

[*Code for single eposide is 296.2x, recurrent episodes is 296.3x.*]

Depressive Disorder—NOS

[*Interviewer: Code this only when there is clinically significant depression with impairment but full criteria for Major Depression, Dysthymia, Adjustment Disorder with Depressed Mood, or Adjustment Disorder with Mixed Anxiety and Depressed Mood are not met.*]

☐ Depressive Disorder, NOS (311)

Bipolar I Disorder: Manic Episode

[*Interviewer: Diagnosis requires that the client has had a distinct period of at least 1 week of abnormally and persistently elevated, expansive, or irritable mood or any period of such mood that resulted in hospitalization; and has had at least three of the symptoms in list B (or four if mood was primarily irritable) to a significant degree. Also the symptoms must create clinically significant impairment in social, academic, or other important areas of functioning, and exclusion criteria must be met.*]

(cont.)

I have some more questions to ask you about your moods or emotional adjustment.

A. Have you ever experienced a period that lasted at least 1 week: [*Enter 1 if present, 0 if absent, and ? if unknown.*]

    1. Where your mood was unusually and persistently elevated; that is, you felt abnormally happy, giddy, joyous, or ecstatic well beyond normal feelings of happiness?   ____

    2. Or where for at least 1 week your mood was abnormally and persistently expansive; that is, you felt as if you could accomplish everything you set your mind to do, were nearly superhuman in your ability to do anything you wished to do, or felt as if your abilities were without limits?   ____

    3. Or where for at least for 1 week your mood was abnormally and persistently irritable; that is you were unusually touchy, too easily prone to anger or temper outbursts, too easily annoyed by events or by others, or abnormally cranky?   ____

    [*Interviewer: If any of above three were endorsed, proceed with B; otherwise, skip to next disorder.*]

B. During the week or more that you showed this abnormal and persistent mood, did you notice any of the following that were persistent and that occurred to an abnormal or significant degree: [*Enter 1 if present, 0 if absent, and ? if unknown.*]

    1. Inflated self-esteem or felt grandiose about yourself well beyond what would be characteristic for your level of abilities   ____

    2. Showed a decreased need for sleep, for instance you they felt rested after only 3 hours of sleep   ____

    3. Were more talkative than usual or seemed to feel pressured to keep talking   ____

    4. Skipped from one idea to another and then another in your speech as if your ideas were flying rapidly by   ____

    Or felt that your thoughts were racing or flying by at an abnormal rate of speed   ____

    5. Were distractible; your attention was too easily drawn to unimportant or irrelevant events or things around you   ____

    6. Showed an increase in goal-directed activity; that is, you became unusually and persistently productive or directed more of your activity than normal toward the tasks you wanted to accomplish   ____

    Or seemed very agitated, overly active, or abnormally restless   ____

    7. Showed an excessive involvement in pleasurable activities that have a high likelihood of have negative, harmful, or painful consequences   ____

    [*Interviewer: If three or more symptoms were endorsed, proceed with remaining criteria; otherwise, skip to next disorder.*]

(cont.)

121

C. [*Enter 1 if present, 0 if absent, and ? if unknown.*]

1. Was this disturbance in your mood enough to cause severe impairment, disruption, or difficulties with social relationships, academic performance, or other important activities ____

2. Or did your abnormal mood lead to your being hospitalized to prevent harm to yourself or others ____

3. Or did you have hallucinations [explain], bizarre ideas [psychotic thinking], or feel or act paranoid (as if others were intentionally out to harm you) ____

D. Exclusion Criteria: [*Interviewer: Enter 1 if symptoms meet criteria for mixed manic–depressive episode or if they are the direct physiological effects of a substance or a general medical condition. Enter 0 if not and ? if unknown. Also, if your client meets criteria for Attention-Deficit/Hyperactivity Disorder, enter 0 only if your client meets the criteria after excluding distractibility (item 4) and psychomotor agitation (second part of 6).*]

Diagnostic Code

Requirements for diagnosis:

Does section A total 1 or more? ____
Does section B total 3 or more? ____
Does section C total 1 or more? ____
Does section D total 0? ____

[Check here if all requirements are met.]
☐ Bipolar I Disorder: Manic Episode (296.xx)
[*Code 296.0x if single episode; 296.40 if multiple episodes and most recent was Manic Episode*]

Bipolar I Disorder: Mixed Episode

[*Interviewer: Code this disorder if criteria are met both for a Manic Episode and for a Major Depressive Episode nearly every day for at least 1 week; disturbance causes clinically significant impairment; and symptoms are not the result of a substance or a general medical condition.*]

☐ Bipolar I Disorder: Mixed Episode (_____)
[*Code 296.6x if most recent episode is mixed, 296.5x if most recent episode is depressed, 296.7 if most recent episode is unspecified.*]

SCHOOL HISTORY

What was the highest level of school that you completed? [*Circle one*]

1. 6th grade or less
2. 7th or 8th grade
5. Some college
6. College graduate

(cont.)

    3. Freshman or sophomore   7. Graduate degree
    4. High school graduate

If you were ever in college, have you ever dropped out of college or stopped   ____
taking courses?

Number of times you have started college courses and failed to complete them.   ____

Did you ever repeat a grade? [Yes = 1, No = 0]   ____
    Which grades did you repeat?_____

Number of times you repeated grades.   ____

Were you ever in any special classes in school? [Yes = 1, No = 0]   ____
    Details:_____

Were you considered a discipline or behavior problem in school? (e.g., a mischief maker   ____
or class clown)?
    Details:_____

Would you say your grades in school were: [Circle one]

    1. A's + B's   3. C's + D's   5. Widely variable
    2. B ı C's   4. D's + F's

Did your teachers always say you were capable of doing much better than you did?   ____
[Yes = 1, No = 0]

Were you ever truant from school? [Yes = 1, No = 0]   ____
    Details:_____

Were you ever expelled or suspended from school?   ____
    Details:_____

Did you have problems getting along with your peers in school?   ____
    Details:_____

_____

_____

Did you ever get in any physical fights at school?   ____
    If yes, how often and during which grades?_____

Did you have any trouble doing homework?   ____

Did you have trouble with reading comprehension?   ____

(cont.)

Briefly describe the kinds of problems you experienced during your school years. When did they begin? _____

_____

_____

Family Psychiatric History

[*Interviewer: Record here the psychiatric problems that may exist among relatives that are biologically related to this client. Place a checkmark in the cell if that disorder is believed to have existed in that relative.*]

Disorders	Children	Siblings	Mother	Father	Others
ADHD symptoms or diagnosis					
LD symptoms or diagnosis					
Mental retardation					
Psychosis/schizophrenia					
Manic–depression					
Major depression					
Suicide					
Anxiety disorders					
Tics/Tourette syndrome					
Alcohol abuse					
Substance abuse					
Inpatient psychiatric treatment					
Epilepsy/seizures					
Other medical problems (note condition):					

_____

Mental Status Notes

(cont.)

Recommendations

[*Interviewer: Note here the recommendations you are going to suggest to this client based on this evaluation. Simply place a checkmark in the appropriate column next to each type of recommendation.*]

Type of recommendation	Yes	No
Education about ADHD		
Individual counseling		
Trial of medication. Type:		
Vocational assessment		
Marriage counseling		
Compensatory behavioral strategies		
Organizational consultant for work related problems		
Substance abuse counseling/treatment		
Coaching		
Neuropsychological evaluation		
Consultation with college/school personnel		
Consultation with employment supervisor/employer		

Other (briefly note):

Diagnostic Summary

[*Interviewer: Note here if client meets DSM-IV criteria for any of the following. Yes = 1, No = 0.*]

____ ADHD Combined

____ ADHD Primarily Inattentive

____ Dysthymia

____ Major Depression (past)

____ Generalized Anxiety Disorder (past)

____ Generalized Anxiety Disorder (current)

____ Obsessive Compulsive Disorder

____ Alcohol abuse

____ Cocaine abuse

____ Antisocial Personality

____ Learning Disability

____ ADHD Primarily Hyperactive–Impulsive

____ ADHD NOS

____ Major Depression (current)

____ Bipolar Disorder

____ Alcohol dependence

____ Cocaine dependence

____ Oppositional Defiant Disorder

____ Other

Forms for Use during Medication Treatment

PHYSICIAN'S CHECKLIST FOR PARENTS

Name_____ **Date of birth**_____ **Current age** ___ **Sex:** M__ F__

Date of evaluation_____Relationship_____

Instructions: This checklist of questions should be reviewed monthly with parents of children taking stimulant drugs.

1. What dose have you been regularly giving to this child over the past month?
   Medication: _____ Dose: _____

2. Have you noticed any of the following side effects this month?

   ☐ Loss of appetite/weight
   ☐ Insomnia
   ☐ Irritability in late morning or late afternoon
   ☐ Unusual crying
   ☐ Tics or nervous habits
   ☐ Headache/stomachache
   ☐ Sadness
   ☐ Rashes
   ☐ Dizziness
   ☐ Dark circles under eyes
   ☐ Fearfulness
   ☐ Social withdrawal
   ☐ Drowsiness
   ☐ Anxiety

3. If so, please describe how often and when the side effects occurred. _____
   _____

4. Have you spoken with the child's teacher lately? How is the child performing in class? _____
   _____

5. Did your child complain about taking the medication or avoid its use? _____
   _____

(cont.)

From *Attention-Deficit Hyperactivity Disorder: A Clinical Workbook* (2nd ed.) by Russell A. Barkley and Kevin R. Murphy. Copyright 1998 by The Guilford Press. Permission to photocopy this form is granted to purchasers of the *Workbook* for personal use only (see copyright page for details).

6. Does the drug seem to be helping the child as much this month as it did last month? If not, what seems to have changed? _____
_____

7. When was your child last examined by the doctor? (If more than 1 year, schedule the child for a clinic visit and exam.) _____
_____

8. Have there been problems in giving the child medication at school? _____
_____

FOLLOW-UP INFORMATION

Name_____ **Date of birth**_____ **Current age**____ **Sex:** M__F__

Medication: _____

Parents' attitudes about medication:_____

Teacher's attitude about medication:_____

Child's attitude about medication:_____

Problems:_____

_____

History

Target symptoms	Improved	No change	Worse
Hyperactivity—motor restlessness			
Attention span			
Distractibility			
Finishing tasks			
Impulse control			
Frustration tolerance			
Accepting limits			
Peer relations			

Side effects	Improved	No change	Worse
Appetite			
Sleep			
Elimination			
Weepiness			
Drowsiness			
Mouth dryness			
Abdominal complaints			
Others: _____			

_____

(cont.)

From *The Handbook of Modern Psychopharmacology*. Copyright 1983 by BMH Clinical Laboratories. Reprinted by permission in *Attention-Deficit Hyperactivity Disorder: A Clinical Workbook* (2nd ed.) by Russell A. Barkley and Kevin R. Murphy. Copyright 1998 by The Guilford Press. Permission to photocopy this form is granted to purchasers of the *Workbook* for personal use only (see copyright page for details).

Physical examination

Height _____

Weight _____

B.P. _____

P. _____

Positive findings_____

_____

WBC _____ Other lab tests: _____ Date done:_____

Impression

_____

_____

_____

_____

_____

R_x_____

Return date: _____

SIDE EFFECTS RATING SCALE

Child's name_____ **Date**_____

Person completing this form_____

Instructions: Please rate each behavior from 0 (absent) to 9 (serious). Circle only one number beside each item. A 0 means that you have not seen the behavior in this child during the past week, and a 9 means that you have noticed it and believe it to be either very serious or occur very frequently.

Behavior	Absent									Serious
Insomnia or trouble sleeping	0	1	2	3	4	5	6	7	8	9
Nightmares	0	1	2	3	4	5	6	7	8	9
Stares a lot or daydreams	0	1	2	3	4	5	6	7	8	9
Talks less with others	0	1	2	3	4	5	6	7	8	9
Uninterested in others	0	1	2	3	4	5	6	7	8	9
Decreased appetite	0	1	2	3	4	5	6	7	8	9
Irritable	0	1	2	3	4	5	6	7	8	9
Stomachaches	0	1	2	3	4	5	6	7	8	9
Headaches	0	1	2	3	4	5	6	7	8	9
Drowsiness	0	1	2	3	4	5	6	7	8	9
Sad/unhappy	0	1	2	3	4	5	6	7	8	9
Prone to crying	0	1	2	3	4	5	6	7	8	9
Anxious	0	1	2	3	4	5	6	7	8	9
Bites fingernails	0	1	2	3	4	5	6	7	8	9
Euphoric/unusually happy	0	1	2	3	4	5	6	7	8	9
Dizziness	0	1	2	3	4	5	6	7	8	9
Tics or nervous movements	0	1	2	3	4	5	6	7	8	9

From *Attention-Deficit Hyperactivity Disorder: A Clinical Workbook* (2nd ed.) by Russell A. Barkley and Kevin R. Murphy. Copyright 1998 by The Guilford Press. Permission to photocopy this form is granted to purchasers of the *Workbook* for personal use only (see copyright page for details).